"In a start-up, founders define the product vision and then use customer discovery to find customers and a market for that vision. Start-ups demand comfort with chaos, uncertainty and change. No business plan survives its first contact with customers."

Steve Blank

DISCIPLINED STARTUP FOUNDER

A FOUNDER'S GUIDE TO CUSTOMER DISCOVERY

ROBERT DE BRUIJN

PATH INSTITUTE

PATH INSTITUTE
The Hague
www.path.institute

Copyright © 2019 Robert de Bruijn
Author: Robert de Bruijn

Publisher: Path Institute
Design: Robert de Bruijn
Illustrations on pages 24, 44, 48, 50, 57, 65, 90, 125, 174, & 178 by freepik.com.

Type of book
ISBN 9789082977806
NUR 801 General Management
BUS025000 Business & Economics: Entrepreneurship

Dedicated to everyone brave enough to face uncertainty.

Book Structure

PREFACE   viii

INTRODUCTION   viii

PART 1   22
Through the Looking Glass dives into questions about starting up.

PART 2   46
Founder's Drive describes the six drive patterns of starters.

PART 3   62
Key Concepts before the Start covers concepts for customer discovery.

PART 4   92
Founders to the Start line describes steps for customer discovery.

PART 5   186
Tools for Working describes key tools for use in your search.

PART 6   204
Glossary covers frequently used terms in start-up land.

DISCIPLINED STARTUP FOUNDER

PART 1

What is a Start-up? **24**

From Start-up to Company **25**

Customer Development Framework **26**

Risk and Uncertainty **28**

Start-up Myths **29**

Double Edge of Domain Expertise **31**

Bigger is Not Necessarily Better **31**

Start a Business not a Start-up **33**

Twitter Case Study **34**

Bootstrapping **36**

Disrupt or Revolutionise **39**

Apple Case Study **40**

Desirable, Feasible, Viable **42**

Emerging Technologies **44**

PART 2

Founder Drive Cards **48**

Product Drive **50**

Resource Drive **51**

Cause Vision Drive **52**

Customer Pain Drive **53**

Diagnosing Malaria Case Study **54**

Problem Drive **56**

Customer Segment Drive **57**

Space X Case Study **58**

Delusional Fantasy Drive **60**

PART 3

Rules of Customer Discovery **64**

Hypotheses into Facts **65**

Problem Space vs. Solution Space **65**

Local Ads on Bikes Case Study **66**

The Customer **68**

Planet Sized Challenges **70**

Customer Jobs-to-be-Done **71**

Netflix Case Study **74**

Salesforce Case Study **78**

Shark Bites & Mosquito Bites **80**

Customer Pains & Gains **81**

Cookie Monsters **82**

Problem-Solution Fit **83**

Cookie Monster Radar **84**

Running Experiments **86**

Pivot or Persevere **86**

Eight Pivots **87**

Market Segment Bowling **89**

False Positives and Negatives **90**

PART 4

A Disciplined Founder's Journey **95**

Founder Drive Instructions **96**

Problem Discovery **98**

Customer Watering Holes **98**

Working Moms Case Study **100**

Three Biggest Problem Conversations **102**

Problem Validation Conversations **104**

Advice Interviews **107**

Follow Up Questions **108**

What Not To Do in Problem Discovery **110**

Zero in on Customer Segment **116**

Cookie Monster Profile **119**

Clustering Insight on Cookie Monster Profile **122**

Would you use it? **124**

Ideate Applications **124**

Painstorm Problem **125**

ShopFloQ Case Study **126**

Root Cause Mapping **130**

Google Case Study **132**

Brainstorm Solutions **136**

The Business Model **137**

Reflectively Case Study **138**

Freshwatch Alternatives **142**

Value Proposition **143**

Calculatour Case Study **144**

Value Proposition Map **148**

Design for Delight **152**

The Solution **153**

Club Eten Case Study **154**

Leap-of-Faith Assumptions **158**

Planning Experiments **160**

Experiment Methods **162**

Revenue Streams **168**

Pricing **170**

Channels **175**

Customer Journey **176**

Market Size **178**

Too Big, Too Small, Just Right **180**

Level Up: Product-Market Fit **184**

PART 5

6 Value Proposition Pitches **188**

Value proposition Canvas **196**

Experiment Validation Board **198**

Test & Learning Cards **200**

Business Model Canvas **202**

PART 6

Glossary **206**

Index **210**

CASE STUDIES

Twitter Case Study **34**

Apple Case Study **40**

Diagnosing Malaria Case Study **54**

Space X Case Study **58**

Local Ads on Bikes Case Study **66**

Netflix Case Study **74**

Salesforce Case Study **78**

Working Moms Case Study **100**

ShopFloQ Case Study **126**

Google Case Study **132**

Reflectively Case Study **138**

Calculatour Case Study **144**

ClubEten Case Study **154**

FEATURE SPREADS

Customer Development Framework **26**

Emerging Technologies **44**

Founder Drive Cards **48**

Cookie Monster Radar **84**

Running Experiments **86**

What Not To Do in Problem Discovery **110**

Clustering Insight on Cookie Monsters **122**

Leap-of-Faith Assumptions **158**

Planning Experiments **160**

Customer Journey **176**

Preface

There are many excellent books for the novice entrepreneur, including Bill Aulet's *Disciplined Entrepreneurship* (to which the title of this book owes more than a small debt), Rob Fitzpatrick's *The Mom Test*, Dan Olsen's *The Lean Product Playbook*, Steve Blank's *The Start-up Owner's Manual,* and Alexander Osterwalder's *Value Proposition Design*. So why add yet another book to the growing pile on the subject? To answer that question requires a small historical tour.

The modern era of the entrepreneurial method was heralded in by Steve Blank in 2005 with *The Four Steps to the Epiphany* and by Eric Ries with *Lean Startup* in 2011. While the four steps sketched the general framework and lean startup covered digital startups and a core idea of validated learning, a lot was left unclear. Steve Blank addressed this partly in 2012 with his second book with co-author Bob Dorf, *The Startup Owner's Manual*. It wasn't until 2014 however that Alexander Osterwalder and Yves Pigneur tied many concepts together in a trail blazing visual style in their second book, *Value Proposition Design*. It was perfectly timed. Start-ups and customer development (the four phase framework developed by Steve Blank in *The Four Steps to the Epiphany*), was hot. Enthusiastically, I gifted several senior business professionals interested in mentoring start-ups a copy of *Value Proposition Design* to familiarise them with the core concepts of validated learning. But a month or two later I was in for a surprise when I checked in on their progress. They praised the book, they said it was stunning; but. A 'but'? The rich visuals had left them a confused, a little at a loss. They weren't sure what to do with it, where to start. How, I wondered, could smart, successful people not get it? As I went through it again, page by page, with a beginner's mindset, a suspicion grew in me. Had I handed a non-linear, non-textual book to people accustomed to linear writing logic, without preparing them for the difference? I called around to see if my suspicions were correct. What did they know about customer development before reading *Value Proposition Design*? What did they already know of contemporary entrepreneurial methods? Very little it turned out. Familiarity with the start-up phenomena came mainly from mainstream media. I checked with several starting founders, their ability to use the book cold and came up with a similar result. It was great for all the design thinker practitioners out there, but for the rest it wasn't all that. For anyone not used to visual thinking, for anyone not acquainted with the language and concepts of lean startup, a book that combined the best of both was difficult to access.

That insight started me thinking about how and what would help starters and mentors who neither had the time nor the patience to master the body of knowledge before getting going. This book is the result. A guide for novice starters, focused to customer discovery concisely, grounded in the actual experience and perspective of diverse founders. It has evolved over the years of crafting it through several iterations with student starters. I have endeavoured to sketch several routes to help the starters overcome mistakes early providing as many aids as strictly necessary. In th process many extant models have been hybridised when it made sense to do so for the sake of simplicity. This book will also support the mentor in discussing the results of customer discovery with a starter. This book is not a complete replacement to all the books mentioned but seeks to simplify and balance textual explanation and visual demonstration.

BOOK MARK

STARTERS

Want to just do it?
Turn the page »

EXPERTS

Want to become
an expert start-up
mentor? Add these
titles to your reading
list and start doing.

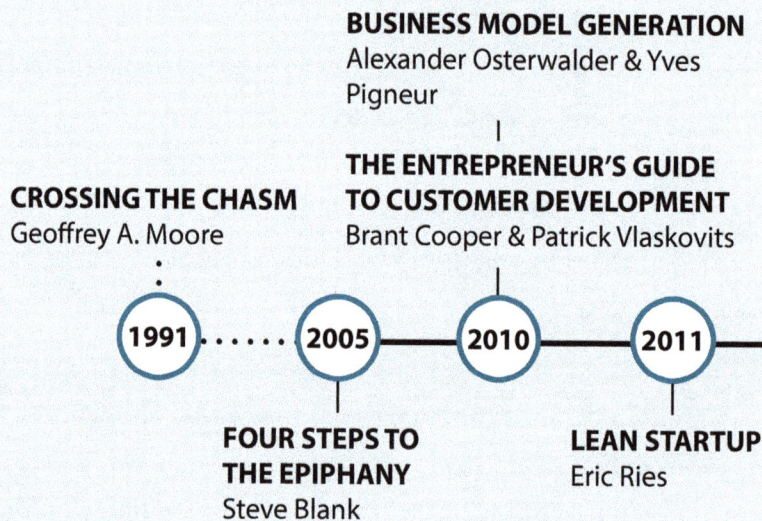

BUSINESS MODEL GENERATION
Alexander Osterwalder & Yves
Pigneur

**THE ENTREPRENEUR'S GUIDE
TO CUSTOMER DEVELOPMENT**
Brant Cooper & Patrick Vlaskovits

CROSSING THE CHASM
Geoffrey A. Moore

1991 · · · · · · 2005 — 2010 — 2011 —

**FOUR STEPS TO
THE EPIPHANY**
Steve Blank

LEAN STARTUP
Eric Ries

THE STARTUP OWNER'S MANUAL
Steve Blank

RUNNING LEAN
Ash Maurya

VALUE PROPOSITION DESIGN
Alexander Osterwalder & Yves Pigneur

LEAN ENTERPRISE
Trevor Owens & Obie Fernandez

DESIGN A BETTER BUSINESS
Patrick van der Pijl, Justin Lokitz, & Lisa Kay Soloman

SPRINT
Jake Knapp, John Zeratsky & Braden Kowitz

2012   **2013**   **2014**   **2015**   **2016**

DISCIPLINED ENTREPRENEURSHIP
Bill Aulet

THE MOM TEST
Rob Fitzpatrick

THE LEAN ENTREPRENEUR
Brant Cooper & Patrick Vlaskovits

SCALING LEAN
Ash Maurya

THE LEADER'S GUIDE
Eric Ries

THE LEAN PRODUCT PLAYBOOK
Dan Olsen

Use this guide when...

You are a starter. Even though every startup is different the process is roughly the same. The big idea behind disciplined startup is that you build little stepping stones like building models and prototypes, running experiments and talking to customers tot get you a little bit closer to the grand vision while it's not too risky for us to go out and actually do.

No one can tell you how to run this business you're founding, you have to figure that out for ourself but in that process of figuring it out and navigating the stepping stones there are patterns and ways that work better and worse. This book points out the stepping stones. It's up to you to step on them, and when you do to create your own learning about *your* customers. We can't, we regret, and don't offer you certainty. Customer discovery helps the starter decide for themselves when something is proven to be true or false, enough that they are willing to risk their own resources, be it time or money, on taking the next step, and the next.

As more and younger starters give it a shot rather than take a position at an established company after graduating, and technology becomes cheaper and promotion of entrepreneurship skyrockets, more and more first-time founders lack any professional domain expertise. This guide is particularly useful for helping you rapidly gain the most important expertise you need.

Novice starters with domain experience will also benefit from this book. Domain experience is most definitely a benefit when it comes to spotting an opportunity, but can bring blind spots through a tendency towards anchoring and confirmation biases with regards to customers real motives and needs.

If a starter is to be successful at not wasting money and opportunity they must:

- Learn to resist building their product before really understanding the customer's struggle.

- Have a strategy that guides them in executing customer development.

- Know when they have learned enough about their customer's struggle to begin creating solutions

- Be able to quickly and easily communicate this information throughout the team.

1

~ through the looking glass ~

Contents

What is a Start-up?   24

From Start-up to Company   25

Customer Development Framework   26

Risk and Uncertainty   28

Start-up Myths   29

Double Edge of Domain Expertise   31

Bigger is Not Necessarily Better   31

Start a Business not a Startup   33

Twitter Case Study: Walking in the Wilderness   34

Bootstrapping   36

Disrupt or Revolutionise   39

Apple Case Study: A Vision of Transparency   40

Desirable, Feasible, Viable   42

Disruptive Business Models & Emerging Technologies   44

What is a Start-up?

A start-up is a temporary organisation, designed to grow fast, that exists to search for a scalable and repeatable business model in the face of uncertainty. A start-up is innovative applying either a new technology, applying old technology in a new way, or applying a new business model. Start-ups displace inferior innovations across markets and industries with new products and business models. Joseph Schumpeter, the twentieth century economist, referred to this as the "gale of creative destruction".

Not all new ventures are start-ups. A SME (small medium enterprise), including but not limited to trading firms, restaurants, retail stores and professional services, are not start-ups. The founders of these are certainly entrepreneurs but they are not start-up founders as SMEs are generally not scalable.

Start-ups differ also from a company in two important respects. Companies have an internal organisation structure and processes that are designed to create and deliver value propositions to known customers. Secondly, companies seek to manage risk and create steady, predictable growth. Start-ups are flat organisations with no permanent structure nor mature processes that seek out uncertainty and rapid scalability. Eric Ries, author of *Lean Start-up*, defines entrepreneurship as "management under extreme uncertainty". Although both big and small enterprises must manage risk only start-up founders must learn to manage uncertainty.

> Startups are temporary organisations designed to search for a repeatable and scalable business opportunity. *Steve Blank*

From Start-up to Company

Embracing uncertainty requires start-ups to have a flat organisation that pivots quickly when customer data requires it. The team is small and there is no formal organisation structure. That doesn't mean there's no organisation just that the team members all know that they are all responsible for success. Steve Blank, serial entrepreneur and author of *The Four Steps to the Epiphany* developed the Customer Development Framework to describe the four stages of how a start-up evolves into a company.

Stage 1 customer discovery, is all about finding what's called a problem-solution fit. Finding a problem important enough for customers to solve and developing a value proposition that they'll love.

Stage 2 customer validation, is all about finding product-market fit. To service the customer reliably you have to figure out a repeatable business model. It should cost less to serve each additional customer to be a scalable business. By this stage you should have a few dozen customers if B2B or a few hundred if B2C.

Stage 3 customer creation, is all about driving a lot more customers through your sales process. In this stage you will work out the bugs of the business processes to serve 10x more customers. Management starts to become more important than entrepreneurship.

Stage 4 company building, is all about standardising processes and creating organisational structures and functional positions. At this stage management is dominant.

Customer Development Framework

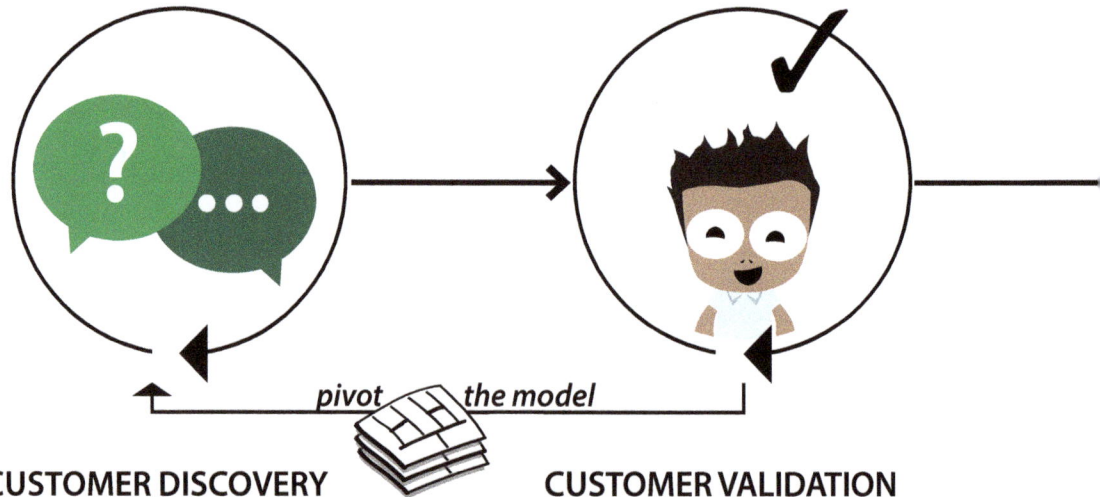

CUSTOMER DISCOVERY
Test the customer problem, customer jobs-to-be-done, pains & gains, and test a valuable solution. Ends when problem-solution fit is achieved.

CUSTOMER VALIDATION
Test problem-solution fit and revenue with a minimum viable product. Ends when the business model is validated and product-market fit is demonstrated with multiple sales to cookie monsters.

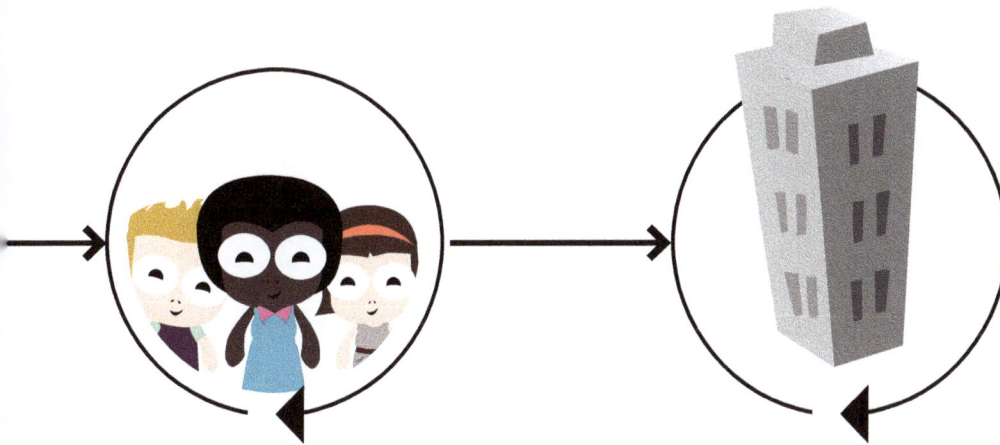

CUSTOMER CREATION
Start building end user demand. Drive customers to your sales channels and begin scaling up activities and resources.

COMPANY BUILDING
Standardise activities and create specialist departments to create and deliver the value proposition at quantrity with consistent quality. Managing risk becomes more important than managing uncertainty.

Risk and Uncertainty

What are the odds that your new idea will succeed? If it does, what will the return to you be? One of the problems in business is that we often can't know the answer to questions like this. In 1921, Frank Knight addressed this dilemma in *Risk, Uncertainty and Profit*. He made the following distinction between risk and uncertainty.

"The practical difference between risk and uncertainty is that with risk the distribution of the outcome in a group of instances is known while in the case of uncertainty that isn't the case the reason being that it's impossible to form a group of instances, because the situation being dealt with is in a high degree unique."

An example of risk is rolling a pair of dice. Before we roll, we know in advance what the odds are for each possible outcome. Managing risk is pretty straightforward. You match up your investment to the odds of it paying off. Managing uncertainty is trickier. Genuine uncertainty is not even knowing the possible outcomes in advance, let alone the probabilities.

Successful companies are good at sustaining innovation which is risky in the sense of the word defined above. Industry leaders are organized to develop and introduce sustaining technologies. Year after year launching new and improved products to gain a competitive advantage. They do so by developing processes for evaluating the technological potential of sustaining innovations and for assessing

You don't have to be an expert on startups to be an entrepreneur, but you do have to be an expert on your customers. *Paul Graham*

their customers' needs. But those same companies seldom introduce—or cope well with—disruptive innovations. Disruptive innovations occur so intermittently that no company has a routine process for handling it. Disruptive innovations create an entirely new market through the introduction of a new kind of product or service.

Large companies often surrender emerging growth markets to smaller, disruptive companies despite having abundant capital and human resources because they lack the organisational capabilities for dealing with genuine uncertainty.

Start-up Myths

There are quite a number of myths around start-up life that we'd like to nip in the bud right away.

You have to fail fast and often to succeed. What a load of crock. The people who keep repeating this like a mantra have forgotten (or never knew) the origins of this idea, namely that building experiments to signal early on when a direction is poor or promising is essential. However, failing i.e. bankruptcy doesn't teach you anything except what not to do. Learn from success; what does work.

You've got to burn the midnight oil to make it. Nonsense. In our culture we seem to take a perverse pleasure in workaholism. We get off on feeling like heroes because we work more than others. But that's just not sustainable. Your decisions aren't likely to be good when overworking for two reasons, you can no longer tell what work really needs to get done urgently. And you end up having nothing but work in your life.

Entrepreneurs are a cool risk devouring breed. Bullshit. Let's retire the word entrepreneur. It's got a dusty old club feel to it. Entrepreneurs do start something. Most without knowing what they're getting themselves into. This is one more of those heroism cults like workaholism. Anyone can start something. So just be a starter.

You need an exit strategy. Why? Are you doing something you don't believe in? If you're thinking how to get out before you've even got going something has got to be wrong.

Go where the big opportunity is. Nonsense, scratch your own itch. Do what you believe in. No one ever became a fan of something that was clearly just about the money.

Just follow your passion. That's stupid and just as damaging as "only go for the big money". Just following your passion isn't all that smart. What you know about and what you can do are *as* important. The best start-ups are; 1) what you believe in - you can see how it could become a real business, 2) what you can do - you have some kind of advantage in addressing the opportunity, 3) what you know - you have some domain expertise.

You need investment to make it. Outside money is addictive, spending it is easy. The best capital is revenue. When you're just beginning you've got no leverage so it's usually a bad deal. It distracts from focusing on the customer, you give up control and have to justify your decisions to investors. Customers move down the totem pole and you wind up building what investors want not what customers want. Investors want their money back cashing-out harming long-term sustainability and building a quality business. Ask yourself how much do you really need? Do you need that office, that logo, that fancy [fill in the blank]?

Double Edge of Domain Expertise

Relative inexperience is both a boon and a bane. It's a boon because what you don't know you don't know won't stop you. It's a bane because what you don't know might kill you (figuratively speaking, of course).

Domain expertise is a benefit when it comes to spotting customer problems. Founders who have identified a real customer problem as a result of experience in a domain have an advantage over founders with just an idea. The latter have a lot of learning to do about the customer problem before thinking about solutions. But there is a flip side. Deeply held assumptions about the customer, because you 'know' what the problem is, cause blind spots that can prevent creating a great solution. An identified customer problem may be indistinguishable from our beliefs about customers and what 'won't' work. Assumptions anchor our thinking and founders with domain expertise have to work just as hard to challenge them.

Bigger is Not Necessarily Better

A unicorn is a legendary creature with a single large, pointed, spiralling horn stuck on its forehead. We're big fans of these unicorns. A unicorn is also that rare

> People are obsessed with big. You shouldn't. Be obsessed with the kind of company you want to create. Make a conscious decision.

start-up that reaches one billion Euro in market capitalization value.

Mark Zuckerberg wrote code for an "on-line facebook within Harvard." Brian Chesky and Joe Gebbia of Airbnb rented air mattresses on their floors and served breakfast to help pay rent. Slack's Stewart Butterfield built a product for his internal team's communication issues. None of these companies started big, and you shouldn't be trying to either. There's a difference between having a vision and trying to make that vision a reality; on day one. Don't do it. The small, focused products that served as version one for Facebook, Airbnb and Slack were manual, incredibly limited and not at all visually appealing, but they were enough to test with customers.

One billion customers start with one. Every product starts with that one customer, like Slack's internal team or Airbnb's first overnight guest. They made sure the experience was that much more perfect for their first customer before worrying about scaling up.

Big things start small. Slack was created to solve a specific problem for a single team that worked closely together. Airbnb started in the founder's apartment as a way to help them afford rent. Global domination wasn't in the cards until later.

Global things start locally. Facebook started as an exclusive social network for Harvard students called "Thefacebook." From there, it expanded to other Ivy Leagues and universities in Boston. More colleges and international reach came much later. Facebook made sure that its product was blowing up locally before expanding its market.

Automated things start manually. In the early days, the Airbnb founders took all the property photos to list on their site. Facebook employees emailed registration invites through an on-line university mailing list. Both companies made sure that their product fulfilled a specific function before putting time and dollars into making individual processes easier and more automatic.

It turns out to be rather difficult to get big. Research of the top hundred software companies in the United States of America revealed it took on average ten years to reach fifty million in revenue. The most successful companies took six years to get to ten million in revenue. Keep in mind that only one in two start-ups even make it to their fifth year let alone have multi-million revenues to show.

Start a Business not a Start-up

To succeed in business, you have to be in business. Don't think of yourself as a start-up founder the first day a business idea hits you. Think of yourself as a starter. Start doing.

You can start doing by talking to people about problems. A great example of this is Martin, an experienced executive in telecommunications, who decided to start a new venture with three colleagues. But they didn't know exactly which business to start. They agreed not to start anything until they had found a problem that was worth solving. Once a week they met to talk about prob-

> The way to get going is to quit talking and start doing.
> *Walt Disney*

TWITTER CASE STUDY
WALKING IN THE WILDERNESS

In July of 2005 Odeo was putting the finishing touches on their startup platform for pod-casting when Apple announced iTunes would include a pod-casting platform. Evan Williams decided the company's future was not in pod-casting, and later that year told the company's 14 employees to start coming up with ideas for a new direction. The company started holding "hackathons" where employees would spend a whole day working on projects.

Odeo co-founder Noah Glass gravitated toward Jack Dorsey, whom Glass says was "one of the stars of the company." Jack had an idea for a completely different product that revolved around "status" — what people were doing at a given time. "He started talking to me about this idea of status and how he was really interested in status," Glass says. "I was trying to figure out what it was he found compelling about it. There was a moment when I was sitting with Jack and I said, 'Oh, I do see how this could really come together to make something really compelling.' We were sitting on Mission St. in the car in the rain. We were going out and I was dropping him off and having this conversation. It all fit together for me."

One day in February 2006, Glass, Dorsey, and a German contract developer Florian

Weber presented Jack's idea to the rest of the company. It was a system where you could send a text to one number and it would be broadcasted out to all your friends. Everyone agrees that Twitter sprang from Jack Dorsey's mind. Dorsey even has drawings of something that looks like Twitter that he made years before he joined Odeo. But all the early employees and Odeo investors also agree that no one at Odeo was more passionate about Twitter in the early days than Noah Glass.

Evan Williams was skeptical of Twitter's potential, but he put Glass in charge of the project. "It was predominantly Noah who pushed for the project to be started," says Blaine Cook, who describes Glass as Twitter's "spiritual leader." "He definitely had a vision for what it was," says Ray McClure.

"There were two people who were really excited [about Twitter]" concurs Odeo investor George Zachary. "Jack and Noah Glass. Noah was fanatically excited about Twitter. Fanatically! Evan and Biz weren't at that level. Not remotely." Zachary says Glass told him, "You know what's awesome about this thing? It makes you feel like you're right with that person. It's a whole emotional impact. You feel like you're connected with that person."

Early on the entire Twitter service was running on Glass' laptop, an IBM Thinkpad. "It was right there on my desk," Glass says, "I could just pick it up and take it anywhere in the world. That was a really fun time."

In August 2006 a small earthquake shook San Francisco and word quickly spread through Twitter — an early 'ah-ha!' moment for users and company watchers alike. By the fall, Twitter had thousands of users. ■

> **Prove an idea has real merit before you think about "starting up". Until then, keep it as a side project.**

lems they encountered and during the week they talked with people in the industry to check their ideas about the problem. Over the next six months they generated many insights but kept pushing for a problem so big that 'you'd need a tourniquet, or die'. Finally, they homed in on the problem of rapidly expanding call centres. After more than a year of investigations, they decided to make the move to start a start-up.

You can start by just selling something. Woot.com began in 2004 as a way for Matt Ruttledge to clear out unsold inventory of electronics. Woot evolved into the first daily deals site and in 2010 Amazon bought Woot for $110 million.

Other founders walk in the wilderness several years before hitting on a scalable business. In 2006 Australian web entrepreneur Dan Norris started a web design agency. Over the next seven years, he made a median income and finally decided to sell the business to invest in a new venture called *Web Control Room*. It bombed. Out of money he launched *WP Curve* offering unlimited small fix jobs to WordPress site owners for a fixed monthly fee. For the next seventeen of nineteen months, the business grew at 8% per month. Wandering in the wilderness involves figuring out how to make money along the way until you've figured out a value proposition customers love and a business model that works.

Bootstrapping

For every 100,000 start-ups only two percent seek external funding. Of those maybe four hundred get it from venture capital funds and ninety from angel groups. Of those backed by venture capital thirty get their money back. The investment rule of thumb is of every ten start-ups invested in two must do well (10x investment), two do okay (return the principle with a little extra), and the rest do terrible. But only about six percent ever go public or go through an M&A – these are the ones that "do well". So when you take investor money the statistically likely outcome is going to be negative, for you. Investors have spread their risk.

The default should be to bootstrap. Bootstrapping is using your own financial resources and money generated from sales to grow a business. As we saw above there is a tendency among start-up founders to seek investment funding to build their product, to cover their personal income needs, to make their lives easier. Here are seven reasons to bootstrap rather than seek angel or venture capital investment.

1. Investors aren't willing to pay your salary.

2. Investors want to see traction and don't like investing in ideas.

3. Investments in ideas with no traction end up taking the lion's share of equity. If you founded the start-up because you wanted to be your own man, you're now handing over the keys to the kingdom before you've even started.

4. What kind of company do you want? It's said that it's better to own a small piece of a big pie than all of a small pie. That can be true if your only reason is to go big and exit. But if you want to build a company, a slower more sustainable growth strategy may be the better choice. When you bootstrap

you can take the time you need and make the decisions that are right for the business, not the investor.

5. Investors want to see their investment increase ten or twenty fold within five years. Let's say you take a €100,000 investment, for your investor to get their return the business must be worth €1,000,000 after five years. That's a lot of pressure. Once you're on the investment gravy train; there's no way off except a new round of investment for investors with less appetite for risk.

6. Founders can be overly optimistic when forecasting their opportunity to investors. This can lead to unpleasant conditions where you end up having to meet investors' needs rather than customers.

7. Angel and venture capital investors have an appetite for risk, but not uncertainty. They're looking to invest in the next, sure, big thing. There's always a hype about some market. An innovator leads and then clones pop up because investors are looking to invest in "something like [big unicorn]". When a founder of a start-up has had success in an area some of the uncertainty is taken out of building similar me-too concepts with a small 'innovative' twist. Do your own thing. Maybe the tornado will hit your industry, and if it does, you will be ahead of the curve and able to dictate investment terms and conditions.

When you have the product plus reference customers plus a working business model and you want (or need) to grow faster, then it's time to seek outside investment. With real traction you will be in a much better position to negotiate equity.

BOOTSTRAPPING FOR NEWBIES

The first key to bootstrapping is finding good mentors. Not just anybody who has a general big business background. Find people who have been there and done that, in your industry, who will tell you what you need to hear even if you don't like what they tell you. Outside investment will bring good things like accountability, for one, and connections, for another. But good, independent mentors who have your best interests at heart can keep you accountable and they can also help you make connections.

The second key to bootstrapping is picking the right business. The right business is something that is not capital intensive. *Space X* is capital intensive. A wind farm in the north sea is capital intensive. The right business is something that will get you paid by your customer up front, not in six months time or a year. If you only get paid six months after delivery you're in a working capital intensive type of business that requires you invest upfront. These are not good businesses for novice founders, and certainly not good for bootstrapping.

Disrupt or Revolutionise

Elon Musk has criticised start-up methods for not generating revolutionary solutions to planetary challenges like clean energy, space exploration, zero waste production, income inequality and disease. In 2017 Mark Zuckerberg exhorted graduates to take on big meaningful projects together. Do unicorns like Facebook actually make the world a better place to live in? Did Elon Musk's PayPal address

APPLE CASE STUDY
A VISION OF TRANSPARENCY

Steve Jobs had a vision of computing that was friendly and easy to use. In late 1979 the twenty-four-year-old entrepreneur paid a visit to Xerox PARC the innovation arm of the Xerox Corporation in Silicon Valley. Nestled in the foothills on the edge of Palo Alto, in a long, low concrete building with enormous terraces looking out over Silicon Valley a visitor to PARC could easily imagine that it was the computer world's lord. At the time, this wasn't far from the truth. In 1970, Xerox had assembled the world's greatest computer engineers and programmers, and for the next ten years had an unparalleled run of innovation and invention. Which was why the young Steve Jobs had driven to Coyote Hill Road.

Apple was one of the hottest tech firms in the country. Everyone in the Valley wanted a piece of it. So Jobs proposed a deal: he would allow Xerox to buy a hundred thousand shares for a million dollars if PARC would "open its kimono." A lot of haggling ensued. Jobs was the fox, after all, and PARC was the hen house. Some at PARC thought that the whole idea was lunacy, but, in the end, Xerox went ahead with it.

One PARC scientist recalls Jobs as "rambunctious". He was given a couple of tours and ended up standing in front of a Xerox Alto, PARC's prized personal computer. An engineer named Larry Tesler conducted the demonstration. He moved the cursor across the screen with the aid of a "mouse". Tesler just clicked on one of the icons on the screen opening and closing "windows," deftly moving from one task to another. He wrote on an elegant word processing program and exchanged e-mails with other people at PARC over the world's first Ethernet network.

"Jobs was pacing around the room, acting up the whole time," Tesler recalled. "He was very excited. Then, when he began seeing the things I could do on-screen, he watched for about a minute and started jumping around the room, shouting, 'Why aren't you doing anything with this? This is the greatest thing. This is revolutionary!'". Jobs raced back to Apple and demanded that the team working on the company's next generation personal computer change course. He wanted menus on the screen. He wanted windows. He wanted a mouse.

He met with Dean Hovey, one of the founders of the industrial-design firm that would become known as IDEO. "Jobs went to Xerox PARC on a Wednesday or a Thursday, and I saw him that Friday afternoon," Hovey recalled. "I had a series of ideas that I wanted to bounce off him, and I barely got two words out of my mouth when he said, 'No, no, no, you've got to do a mouse.' I was, like, 'What's a mouse?' I didn't have a clue. So he explains it, and he says, 'You know, [the Xerox mouse] is a mouse that cost three hundred dollars to build and it breaks within two weeks. Here's your design spec: Our mouse needs to be manufacturable for less than fifteen bucks. It needs to not fail for a couple of years, and I want to be able to use it on Formica and on my blue jeans.'" From that meeting, I went to Walgreens, which is still there, at the corner of Grant and El Camino in Mountain View, and I wandered around and bought all the underarm deodorants that I could find because they had that ball in them. I bought a butter dish. That was the beginnings of the mouse."

Steve Jobs created the highest valued business in the 21st century with borrowed technology that fulfilled his vision for transparent, easy to use computing. That vision brought the graphic user interface to desktop computers and later the iPod, the iPad and the iPhone. ∎

c:\>d

a planetary scale challenge? Only a small percentage seem to be making a 'big dent' in the universe when looked at from this perspective. But is that because of start-up methodologies or the result of a dearth of vision, or an excess of exit strategies, or both? Or is it that many start-up founders are under thirty who need time to incubate a big vision and ambition and first learn the ropes before being revolutionary?

To be disruptive a start-up founder must first identify an under-served customer; a customer who experiences a problem but for whom current solutions are either too complex or too costly. Second the start-up founder must develop a solution that is less costly or less complex. PayPal and Facebook were both highly disruptive. Revolutionary innovation on the other hand, often involves developing or implementing game changing technology. The road to technology readiness can be long and expensive. For example; a breakthrough in materials sciences leads to a new solar cell that is 200% more efficient than existing cell technologies. But the production process for this new type of cell still has many complicated steps making the new technique commercially uncompetitive. With enough development the revolutionary technique can be brought to market. But it will take patience and money, lots of money. There is actually no lack of start-ups tackling big challenges, they're just not the media darlings of Silicon Valley.

Desirable, Feasible, Viable

For innovation to be called successful a solution must be both desirable from a human point of view, feasible from a technological point of view, and viable from an economic point of view. We focus very much on discovering the desirability of a solution but by no means does that mean we forget that feasibility and viability are equally important.

If something is economically viable is in part a question of the price premium you will be able to generate of the value you create and the cost which is incurred in creating and delivering your value proposition. This is a challenge for you in the customer validation stage, not the customer discovery stage that this book focuses on.

If something is technologically feasible is simple to determine. The only question is: "does the technology already exist?". If the answer is "no" you are probably fantasizing science fiction technology. Teleportation makes for great movie situations but is not technically feasible (nor theoretically feasible for that matter), today. Perhaps one day scientists will discover laws of the universe that does enable teleportation but until that day it remains in the realm of science fiction. It cannot be an answer to a clean transport solution today. The hyper loop, on the other hand, is technically feasible, at least in theory. We know about magnetic levitation. We can create tubes of strong material and de-pressurize them. We can create an airtight capsule that rides magnetic waves. Separately all these things are technologically feasible. It's just that no one has completely, successfully and safely put the pieces together to create a real hyper loop train. The technology is there but will need further development until it is also economically viable.

DISRUPTIVE BUSINESS MODELS
& EMERGING TECHNOLOGIES

It's not just innovative products or services that create disruptive businesses. Revenue stream, channel and partnerships innovation also lead to bold new ways of serving existing customer jobs. Assets originally produced to be sold are "servitised" through lease, rent or usage fees. You might do your laundry at a laundromat for example, or lease a car. Increasingly, subscription revenue models are applied to software over the web. Both Salesforce and Netflix applied subscription revenue models and web technology to make the value proposition less costly, less cumbersome, and less complex. AirBnB, Uber and a whole spate of new companies have crowd-sourced not just finances or user content, they've co-opted the very physical assets of customers. The customers are truly partners in many respects co-creating the value of the platforms these businesses establish.

And then there are many exciting developments in emergent General Purpose Technologies, like the Internet. We present a few of the more recent entrants that have already established a beachhead in commerce. Each represents a major opportunity for disruptive innovation.

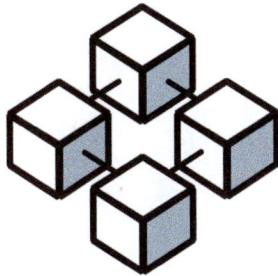

Blockchain, a distributed ledger system which has as big a potential as relational databases to enable new ways of accomplishing transactions between parties.

CRISPR, a gene editing technique that allows existing genes to be removed and/or new ones added much more easily than earlier techniques. This has many potential applications, including medicine and crop seed enhancement. The use of CRISPR/Cas9 for genome editing was the American Association for the Advancement of Science's choice for breakthrough of the year in 2015.

Robotics, machine learning & augmented intelligence, autonomous vehicles are hot topics. Robotics has long since gone beyond the factory floor. But robotics doesn't only refer to physical systems it also refers to smart systems able to learn and adapt to their environment, to experiment. Web chatbots are an example of limited machine learning dealing with routine customer queries today.

Additive (3D) manufacturing, using lasers to print materials from plastics to steel and even organics, 3D manufacturing can use less materials, can make batches as small as one, and print objects that aren't possible to manufacture with conventional technologies.

2

~ founder's drive ~

Contents

Founder Drive Cards   48

Product Drive   50

Resource Drive   51

Cause Vision Drive   52

Customer Pain Drive   53

Diagnosing Malaria Case Study   54

Problem Drive   56

Customer Segment Drive   57

Space X Case Study   58

Delusional Fantasy Drive   60

FOUNDER DRIVE

What's your drive? There are six patterns to startup origins we call the *founder's drive*. These patterns describe the founder's initial motivation to start the journey.

USE A DRIVE CARD TO NAVIGATE YOUR CUSTOMER DISCOVERY JOURNEY.

CUSTOMER PAIN DRIVE

I keep running into the same problem time and time again. It's got big potential! I need to figure out a solution that can be a business.

Example
always throwing away lots of fresh food

RESOURCE DRIVE

I've got this breakthrough tech that's the best thing since the wheel was invented; it's got so many applications. I just have to figure out customer problems I can solve with it. Who needs it and what for?

Example
blockchain

PROBLEM DRIVE

I just want to start a business that can scale. I'm looking for any customer jobs that need a tourniquet!

SEGMENT DRIVE

I want to help improve the lives of a particular group of people. I need to figure out what they need help with the most.

Example
single working mothers

PRODUCT DRIVE

I've got an idea for a product that's the best thing since sliced bread! I think it can be a real business. I've just got to figure out who wants or needs it.

Example
local ads on student bikes

VISION CAUSE DRIVE

I'm passionate about a cause and am inpired to act. I need to understand what stakeholder's problems are worth solving and that I have an advantage in solving. Peace sells, but who's buying?

Example
eradicating malaria

PRODUCT DRIVE

The most common drive is a product drive. Product driven founders start with an idea for a solution either a product or a service. In today's world this is frequently a mobile application for example for personal finances or a mobile-physical service such as AirBnB. Today it seems there's an app for everything you can imagine, and a whole lot more. Physical product inventions are the second most frequently occurring product driven starts. Many such starts have a major weak point; the founder doesn't have a clear view of who will need or want it. "Everyone" is not a customer and thus it is the highest priority to discover who would want the solution and in which context.

RESOURCE DRIVE

The resource drive comes in three major flavours; technology, human, and information capital. Technology is the most common resource driving engineers and scientists. Such founders start with a technological breakthrough developed in laboratories. We include both hardware such as electronics, photonics, nanotech, and energy harvesting, software such as neural networks and, 'wetware' such as psychology theories. Alternatively, founders may possess some other resource such as skills or information they are intent on levering.

The resource will have many possible applications in several industries. The challenge is to find the right application for the resource. Imagine a caveman showing his new invention - the wheel - to friends. They shrug their shoulders. A wheel: big deal. He returns later with two wheels attached to an axle with square pltform on top and rocks piled high. He's found his first application - transporting construction materials. They 'get' it.

CAUSE VISION DRIVE

The cause vision drive is a vision of the future without a clear idea of a solution such as eradicating malaria in Africa. The hyper loop is an example of a vision; fast, cheap, clean transportation paired with the idea for a solution; a de-pressurised tube, a cabin to hold people, and magnetic levitation for propulsion. Can you think of other ways to achieve the vision of fast, cheap, clean transportation that is feasible with contemporary technologies? Linux, the personal computer operating system, is a vision of open-source software and thus had an unfair advantage in the open-source community from which it sprung. Steve Jobs had a vision of transparent computing. He was a master at applying existing technologies such as the GUI (Graphic User Interface) and the computer mouse, seen at Xerox PARC, to the Apple Lisa (1983) and Macintosh (1984). In 2007 Apple improved on and applied touch screen technology, first patented in 1965, to the iPhone. If you have a vision but no clear idea of a solution you must find the technology to make your vision a reality. You must also discover whether your value proposition is desirable, and if it is financially viable.

CUSTOMER PAIN DRIVE

The next most common drive is the customer pain drive. These founders start with a problem they experience themselves or see others run into. This is also called market pull innovation. Developing a solution to serve this problem seldom requires developing new technology. The founders use existing technologies in new ways to help the customer achieve the desired outcome. When new technology is needed to solve the customer job you face a steep challenge and high capital investment requirements. Think about coming back to this opportunity when you have more experience and capital.

DIAGNOSING MALARIA CASE STUDY
WHICH STAKE-HOLDER TO HELP

We squash mosquitoes with our big hands. We poison-bomb them from spray trucks and airplanes. We irridiate them, drain their habitats, breed them experimentally in laboratories to confound their DNA. Yearly, almost half a million people die from malaria, just one of the serious diseases carried by mosquitoes. Malaria is a complex problem with many possible stakeholders, not least of which is the affected population. Other stakeholders include doctors in big urban hospitals, rural clinic staff, village chemists, and World Health Organisation researchers. Any one of the stakeholders could be a customer. We can probably all generate several ideas to help any or several of the stakeholders get their job done from the simple to the fantastic; cheap mosquito nets (works only while under it), mass insecticide spraying (health hazard), new drugs (expensive), genetically engineer a sterile mosquito (expensive and difficult).

In 2018 Ph.D. candidate Ternitope Agbana and his colleague Hai Gong received an award for their project to diagnose malaria with an adapted smart phone. Having grown up in Nigeria, Agbana is well aware of the problem village chemists face diagnosing malaria. The correct diagnosis of malaria is crucial.

But in practice, it often goes awry. Proper diagnosis requires expensive microscopes only available in main city hospitals. Imagine a small shop in an African village stacked with boxes of pills and potions. People visit the chemist with their complaints and leave with medication.

Under a microscope, malaria shows up in infected red blood cells. A dark spot surrounded by a lighter ring is a tell-tale sign. The World Health Organisation recommends the inspection of 100 microscopy stills of one person's sample to make a correct diagnosis. So even with a microscope, diagnosing malaria takes time and effort. If treated well and on time, a patient can recover within a week. But when misdiagnosed as the flu, malaria will continue to develop in the patient with severe and possibly critical consequences. For example, when a child in rural Nigeria has a fever the community health worker may surmise that the patient has malaria just by feeling the child's temperature with his hand. But all too often the diagnosis is incorrect, and the wrong medication is administered, either because the child's particular strain of malaria has not been identified, or the child doesn't have malaria at all. Because malaria medicines are quite cheap it is often prescribed just-in-case, increasing strain resistance to current medicines. It is the chemist who should be able to reliably diagnose malaria. The technology should be cheap and simple enough to function within this context.

"Of course, the chemist should be able to charge a modest fee for the diagnosis. Otherwise, he is better off selling people medicines regardless of their needs," says Agbana.

Agbana's solution, a smart phone with a small glass ball in front of the camera lens transforms the smart phone into a modest microscope (8.5 X). The built-in zoom function increases the magnification sufficiently to detect the rings in an infected blood sample. It's still early days for the malaria detection tool. Agbana has plenty of ideas to improve the current set-up. For instance, he'd like to be able to detect infected cells without staining the sample. He is also considering using a fluorescent dye to make detection easier and more reliable. Additionally, he is looking into ways of enlarging the field of vision to reduce the required number of stills.

PROBLEM DRIVE

Least common is the problem drive illustrated by the story of Martin in the section Start a Business, not a Start-up above. The drive of the founder is to start a scalable business, period. It is more often experienced founders that take this route. These founders are looking for a business opportunity first and foremost, not something that they love, but something that can be scaled quickly. They are very savvy business people and will consider the exit strategy as a part of the equation when identifying promising opportunities.

CUSTOMER SEGMENT DRIVE

The customer segment drive is similar to a vision cause drive but focuses on a very particular group of people whom the founder is ardent about. To avoid confusion here "people in sub-Saharan Africa exposed to malaria risk" is not a clear segment. For customer segment driven founder's the focus is much more specific and generally results from observations of a group in their personal sphere. For example the troubles experienced by adult children providing home care for elderly parents while working full time, or the struggle of single working mothers, or the struggle of a people with diabetes type II to maintain a lifestyle that prevents progression of the disease to type I.

SPACE X CASE STUDY
A DREAM OF DESTINY

In 2001, Elon Musk conceived "Mars Oasis", a project to land a miniature experimental greenhouse on Mars in an attempt to regain public interest in space exploration. Musk, influenced by Isaac Asimov's novels, views space exploration as an important step in preserving human life.

In October 2001, Musk travelled to Moscow with Jim Cantrell and Adeo Ressi to buy refurbished ICBMs that could send the envisioned payloads into space. The group met with companies such as NPO Lavochkin and Kosmotras but Russian scientists regarded them as novices and the group returned empty handed. In February 2002 the group returned to Russia accompanied by Mike Griffin who had worked for the CIA's venture capital arm and NASA's Jet Propulsion Laboratory. The group met again with Kosmotras and were offered one rocket for US$8 million. Musk believed this was too expensive and stormed out of the meeting. On the flight back calculated that the raw materials for building a rocket were only 3 percent of the sales price of a rocket and realised he could start a company to build the rockets he needed.

Space Exploration Technologies, or SpaceX, was founded in June 2002 with

US$100 million of his own money. With the long-term goal of creating a "true space faring civili-sation" SpaceX develops and manufactures space launch vehicles to advance rocket technology and reduce the cost of human space flight by a factor 10. In 2016 interview, he stated that the first unmanned flight of the Mars Colonial Transporter (MCT) spacecraft would launch in 2022, with the first manned MCT Mars flight departing in 2024. ■

DELUSIONAL FANTASY DRIVE

In the novels of Miguel de Cervantes the titular antagonist Don Quixote does not see the world for what it is but prefers to imagine that he is living out a knightly story. Unfortunately, the start-up founder equivalent of Don Quixote is all to common. People walking around with imaginary technology to power new products that no one wants. People walking around with the glow of moral righteousness, kept warm by the thought of the great social justice they are championing. The latter is mere hubris, the former foolhardiness. Don't be a Don Quixote (non)starter.

3

~ key concepts before the start ~

Contents

Rules of Customer Discovery   64

Hypotheses and Facts   65

Problem Space vs. Solution Space   65

The Customer   68

Planet Sized Challenges   70

Customer Jobs-to-be-Done   71

Shark & Mosquito Bites   80

Customer Pains & Gains   81

Cookie Monsters   82

Problem-Solution Fit   83

Cookie Monster Radar   84

Running Experiments   86

Pivot or Persevere   86

Eight pivots   87

Market Segment Bowling   89

False Positives and Negatives   90

Rules of Customer Discovery

Rule #1: The first rule of customer discovery is; do not talk about your idea.

Rule #2: The second rule of customer discovery is; do not talk about your idea.

Rule #3: The third rule of customer discovery is; don't speak to just any random passer by.

Rule #4: It's not a survey, it's a conversation to discover more.

Rule #5: Explore with your interviewee how they experience things. Adopt a beginner's mindset and probe unexpected information.

Rule #6: Spend twice as much time listening as you do talking. We have two ears and one mouth; your job is to learn, not to inform.

Rule #7: Ask questions rooted in past experience; get facts not hypotheticals. Ask, "Would you describe for me the last time you ...?" not "Would you buy a product that did X?", or "What would you be willing to pay for X?".

Rule #8: Keep the door open and get permission to keep in contact.

Rule #9: Open new doors. Ask for other contacts they feel you should talk to.

Hypotheses and Facts

Start-up founders don't have a lot of facts. They have a lot of hypotheses which is just a fancy word for assumptions. An even simpler word is guesses. Start-up founders have guesses about customers, guesses about solutions and value propositions, about channels, revenue and pricing, about key resources needed and partners to work with. In short an awful lot of guesses (if they've stopped to think about many of the above at all). But guesses are a great place to start doing as Walt Disney advised - quit talking and start doing.

Just be prepared to do one thing, and one thing only. Be ready to kill your darlings. Those assumptions you hold so dear about customers, solutions and the business - you have to be prepared to challenge them and scrap them when the evidence shows you you're wrong. Then you'll be turning hypotheses into facts on which to build. The faster you can do this, the greater your learning velocity and the faster you will be in a position to build a solution and business that customers love.

Problem Space vs. Solution Space

Problem space is where all customer problems that you could aim to solve live. Any product that you build exists in solution space, as do all mock-ups and prototypes. When you conceive of a product, these assumptions exist is solution space. When you build a product, you make choices about how the product looks,

LOCAL ADS ON BIKES CASE STUDY
SOLUTION WITH- OUT A PROBLEM

The founders of Project A enthusiastically started on their big idea - placing local advertisements on student's bikes. They first approached cafe owners believing cafe owners struggled with reaching their target audience. After a week's worth of interviews they discovered that cafe owners didn't advertise, at all. They pivoted to independent store owners only to discover these potential customers had no budget to advertise. Disappointed, they returned home concluding the big idea would not work. But what was the big idea in fact? To put ads on bikes? That's a 'what', not a 'why'. The big idea could be formulated as 'help small retail businesses in the city centre attract customers'. While that would be pretty good it turns out the team really wanted to help students earn a little extra cash and the first idea had been by placing ads on their bikes. Formulating the big business idea as 'enabling students to earn passive, incremental income' would enable a wider number of solutions to be considered after the first, placing local ads on their bikes, proved infeasible. By defining a solution as the big idea the team anchored themselves making any other solution unthinkable and ended up despondent when the solution turned out to be a bust. ■

how it works, and what it does. Your guesses about the solution exist in solution space until you validate them. Until you test them to breaking point asking the questions to the answers you don't want to hear. When you succeed in avoiding deluding yourself the solution you build will be solidly rooted in problem space.

The Customer

"The purpose of a business", asserted Peter Drucker a leading management scholar of the twentieth century, "is to create a customer." A customer is always a living, breathing person. A company is never a customer. Customers are either operating on their own private interests (consumers), or they are operating on behalf of an organisation. While all customers operating on behalf of an organisation are also consumers they will wear only one of these hats at a time. For example, I can buy a new smart phone for my own personal use or I can buy smart phones for business use by all employees in a company. In both instances different things will be of interest and value to me. I'll have different criteria for buying.

When targeting customers who are operating on behalf of an organisation describe them with their function title, for example a 'product marketer in a mid-sized FMCG company'. Always think of the living, breathing person you are seeking to address. Never make the mistake of thinking of business customers as 'company X'. When targeting consumers describe them with a few characteristics such as 'single mothers in the Netherlands'. When you are less specific simply saying mothers or marketers, you're making it a lot harder for

The purpose of business is to create a customer. *Peter Drucker*

yourself to get any early success. Why? Read the section on Cookie Monsters to find out.

Regardless if your customer is a consumers or the agent of an organisation they will take one of three roles: the *user*, the *buyer*, or the *decision maker*. Without giving it much thought we tend to think of the customer as someone who buys and uses the product. Now in the example of the smart phone as a private user that was true but equally, I might be buying the smart phone for a child's use. And in the example of buying it for employees I may or may not be using one of the smart phonesmyself. But I am making the decision on which smart phone model to get in all three cases. There is a scenario in which which user, buyer and decider hats are all worn by different people. Can you see it? Suppose I control the money and have determined how much a smart phone may cost. Someone else determines the technical specifications that the smart phone should live up to and indicates the model to buy and I put through the purchase order. When the phone is delivered the person or persons for whom it is intended take the phone into use. This description could apply equally to a business or to a family. Sometimes a customer wears all three hats at the same time while on other times the hats are worn by different people.

Each customer role has a different interest when it relates to the same offering. Each customer role requires a distinct value proposition catering to their specific interests. For example, the end user of a software application wants to easily enter and retrieve information. The decider must evaluate the application on the best fit with other systems. The buyer must evaluate the application on cost/benefit. Or take as an example buying a family car. The parents are likely to be the decision makers and buyers, while one of the two is likely to be the primary user. A maximum budget will most likely have been agreed up front by both acting as buyer. Total cost of ownership, ecological impact and mileage may also be buyer criteria. As user the father might be primarily interested in power and acceleration, the mother in space and comfort, and the children in digital compatibility and electricity availability. It will be obvious that in order to cater to all to be 'best fit, best price, best solution' requires different value propositions to persuade each customer and role.

Planet Sized Challenges

Big, meaningful challenges; global warming, poverty, inequality, food waste, rising obesity, pollution, decreasing trust in institutions, the accelerating pace of change. These are planet sized problems but not customer problems in the start-up sense. Just as 'a company' cannot be your customer neither can 'society' be a customer. That's not to say that living, breathing customers do not feel the effects of these problems. Societal or organisational problems may shape the space in which you want to make a difference as an entrepreneur. As a start-up founder you can identify and solve a piece of the puzzle by serving a real customer problem or establish a charity that raises funds to campaign or lobby for the cause (but that's an entirely different journey than this book).

Ask yourself who does this affect? What problems are created for them? Why are they struggling now? For example, operations managers of factories are trying to reduce carbon dioxide emissions to meet new regulations. They may have trouble understanding the regulations, they may not know about available technologies or measures to take, or are unable to make the business case to their superiors to get approval. These are all problems that are tangible and addressable by a business.

Customer Jobs-to-be-Done

Peter Drucker wasn't familiar with the theory of customer jobs-to-be-done. If he had, he would have immediately understood the clarity with which this method 'creates a customer'. Until now we've talked about customer problems as a convenient short hand way. We'll now introduce the notion of a job the customer is striving to get done as a more refined way to think about customer problems. Everyday, in our private and professional lives, we try to get specific things accomplished. Some things are small like 'pass the time while waiting in line', some are big like 'change career at 40'. Some are practical like 'retain customers when their mobile phone contract ends'. Some are unpredictable like 'dress for an out-of-town business meeting after the airline lost my luggage' and others are regular like 'pack a healthy lunch for my children in the morning'.

As a theory, customer jobs offers a simple but powerful insight: customers don't buy products, they pull them into their lives to make progress on a job in a certain context. We say that the customer hires (or pulls) the product into

Customers don't buy products, they pull them into their lives to make progress on a job. People don't want to buy a quarter inch drill. They want a quarter-inch hole.
Theodore Levitt

their lives to help them accomplish the task or job. We call these things that people want to get done *customer jobs*, or jobs-to-be-done. The full set of products we consider hiring can go beyond just commercially offered solutions. For example, when preparing income taxes a customer can hire the services of a certified public accountant, use tax preparation software, or just calculate the tax return themselves using a pencil and calculator. When using the solution leads to a satisfying outcome the next time the customer is confronted with the same job they tend to hire that product again. If it does a poor job, customers tend to fire it and look for an alternative.

JOB CONTEXT

The context of a job is whatever set of circumstances within which the customer seeks to achieve the job. This goes beyond simple physical or geographical context, for example the life-stage, the personal relationships, and the financial situation of the customer, to name just a few.

FUNCTIONAL, EMOTIONAL AND SOCIAL JOBS

Customer jobs are functional, emotional or social. For example, we hire a smart phone for the functional job of staying in contact while away from home or the office; to make phone calls, to send messages, to send emails, to keep our day organised, to look things up on the web. It's quite easy to list the features that are there to help us get functional jobs done. A more specific functional job all mobile phones help us get done is capturing and sharing moments using the camera. When such moments are shared with friends and family a deeper emotional job is served for those with whom the moment is shared - feeling connected with loved ones *in the moment experienced.* Emotional jobs and social jobs are less easy to identify and to satisfy. Emotional jobs include things like feeling safe, feeling appreciated, feeling proud, or belonging. Social jobs include getting recognition or status. If you own a top end smart phone or a real techy smart phone you are (unawares) signalling a social status using the phone to satisfy a social job, such as having someone compliment you on your phone. Equally, when a MacBook user opens their laptop at a cafe to work that glowing little Apple logo on the cover signals their social status as an aficionado, a person with taste in fine technology.

When we look at smart phones in the market through this lens we realise how different phones fulfil different peoples emotional or social jobs. iPhone users don't use an iPhone merely to get functional jobs done. They enjoy the industrial design, a feeling of pride in ownership. There is also a coolness factor that Apple imparts, a social signalling of being someone who belongs to that class of people who can really appreciate the finer things in life like the marriage of great design and technology. A Google Pixel phone user signals that the user is tech savvy, cares more about the smart things in a phone like lightweight operating system, speed and power of the phone. A Fairphone user signals their concern for the environment and also a fair measure of tech savvy-ness since the phone is modular.

JOB STATEMENTS AND STORIES

A *job statement* is a simple way to formulate a customer job. The structure of a job statement is: *verb - object - context*. For example,

» Pass time while waiting in line.

NETFLIX CASE STUDY
SURFING DIS-
RUPTION

When Netflix first appeared in the late 1990's it only appealed to movie buffs who didn't care about new releases, early adopters of DVD players and online shoppers. Launching a DVD mail-in subscription service the founders weren't looking to compete head-on in the video rental market dominated by big chains like Blockbuster that had ruled the market throughout the 1980s and 1990s.

Netflix enabled subscribers to create an account and a rental wish list on their website of DVDs they wanted to watch and mailed these through the US postal service. Subscribers could keep DVDs as long as they wanted without any late fines, but could only have a limited number of videos in their possession at any one time. When a DVD was returned by post, Netflix would automatically send the customer the next DVD on their wish list. Using viewing history from the website they were also able to pioneer digital recommendations levering a large library of old titles and displacing demand of new titles.

This changed with the rise of video streaming. Having created their own blue ocean the company was doing well, but realized that past success is no guarantee for the future. Already a player on the market, Netflix launched a new business model streaming video through Amazon Web Services. They moved up in the market appealing to Blockbuster's core audience providing a wider selection of content with an all-you-can-watch, on demand, low-price, high-quality value proposition. ■

- » Change career at 40.

- » Retain customers at contract end.

- » Dress for a business meeting when out-of-town and luggage is lost.

- » Listen to music when running.

- » Pack lunch for kids during hectic morning.

A *job story* is a more elaborate form of a job statement. The structure of a job story is: *the context - the job - the expected outcome*. For example;

- » *When* customers' contracts are ending *I want to* talk to them personally *so I can* increase retention, beat my target and get that bonus.

- » *When* I'm waiting in line *I want to* reduce my boredom *so that* time passes more quickly.

- » *When* I'm stuck in my job *I want to* discover my talents *so I can* take a new direction confidently.

- » *When* I'm out-of-town for a business meeting and the airline lost my luggage *I want to* look sharp and feel powerful *so I can* close the deal.

- » *When* I'm jogging *I want to* get in a rhythm *so I can* make my distance and feel proud.

- » *When* I'm packing my kids lunches in the morning *I want to* create an easy, healthy meal *so I can* feel like a good dad.

EXISTING, UNDERSERVED AND NEW JOBS

Most customer jobs have been around for years. We call these *existing* jobs and all existing jobs are served in some way or other either by home grown solutions or by commercially available solutions. Customers may not be entirely satisfied by the solutions they are currently hiring to get the job done and may be on the lookout for alternatives that perform better.

Some jobs are *underserved*. When saying that a job is underserved we mean that there are customers who are trying to get the job done but they aren't consuming current market solutions. Frequently the reason for their non-consumption is that market solutions are either too costly or too complex for them to gain access to the market. In other words, non-consumption comes about because the barriers to market access for a specific customer segment are too high.

Once in awhile *new* jobs appear on the scene. New jobs are usually a result of technological, regulatory or social change. For example, until the mid 1990's marketers had been accustomed to using print, billboards, radio and television to do their marketing communication. The second half of the 1990's saw the World Wide Web go mainstream and marketers were suddenly confronted with a new medium for marketing which they didn't understand. By the end of the 1990's e-commerce started to get deeper penetration confronting marketeers not just with a new medium for marketing communication but also a new sales channel and extra competition from new online players. At the same time they had to adapt to search engine marketing and advertising to get the attention of web users. Just as marketers were getting a handle on these new jobs with new services created to help them get the jobs done, along came social media which unleashed a Pandora's box of new jobs. These new jobs spawned an entire new industry of

SALESFORCE CASE STUDY
UNDERSERVED SME JOBS

In an era when CRM systems were predominated by global vendors including SAP, IBM, Oracle and Microsoft, who delivered software on CD-ROM that required user licence fees among a dizzying array of pricing schemes, which was complex, powerful and expensive, that required a squad of IT consultants to install and customise to your business Salesforce.com Salesforce.com substituted the CD-ROM installed application client / intranet technology with TCP/IP and web browser based technologies introducing a basic, simple, web-based CRM that was out-of-the-box ready to use, enabled almost no customisation, updated automatically, and used a subscription based payment model for a much lower price to make a CRM system available to a wider audience of small business owners which often comprise up to fifty percent of all businesses in many western economies.

Large customers that bought the incumbent technologies were not interested in Salesforce.com's offering. It didn't provide them with the features they needed, but they weren't the customers Salesforce.com was targeting. They targeted small and medium sized enterprises that couldn't afford the offerings of the giants and didn't need all that power and complexity. Salesforce entered the market for CRM serving SMEs who couldn't afford the complex, CD based, CRMs from Oracle et al., didn't need all the features, and couldn't maintain the IT server infrastructure required to host such solutions at the time.

Salesforce.com was both innovative and proved to be disruptive. They innovated, not by differentiating themselves on a critical success factor within the existing industry, but through identifying an underserved market and developing a cheaper value proposition tailored to the SME needs. Note, it wasn't a low-cost competitive offering either - it was value priced at a price point accessible to many SMEs.

Salesforce was one of the first software to be sold as a service and to run through a web browser even in the days when ISDN connections were not standard. Yet it found a hungry audience in the SMEs who did want to be able track and manage their relations with customers, but needed a simple out-of-the-box solution. Today Salesforce.com is the market leader at 19.7% of the market in an industry worth $26 billion in 2016 (1). It's SaaS business model has supplanted the traditional CRM vendors such as SAP, Microsoft, and Oracle. ■

service providers creating new solutions to help marketers get their marketing jobs done in the era of social media.

Understanding a customers' job is about clustering insights into a coherent story. It's not about statistics. It's about gaining a deep understanding of why someone is seeking to achieve an outcome, why they are struggling currently and what they appreciate in alternative solutions.

SHARK BITE PROBLEMS	MOSQUITO BITE PROBLEMS
Customers are actively trying to solve the problem.	Doing nothing is a viable option.
Customers are actively looking for a solution.	The status quo is preferred above looking for a solution.
Customers have budget earmarked for the problem & want to pay you.	Solutions are "nice to have".
Customers give you all their attention and focus.	It's difficult to get meetings with customers to discuss the problem.
Customers ask a lot of questions and want to be kept informed about next steps.	There's no owner of the problem.

Shark & Mosquito Bites

In the language of start-ups customer jobs are often referred to as either shark bite problems or mosquito bite problems. When a mosquito bites few people will rush out to the pharmacy to buy salve and bandages. But when bitten by a shark those same peoplen will probably do anything for a tourniquet.

Problems come not only in all sizes but also in all frequencies. A single mosquito bite may not be a bother but frequent, multiple mosquito bites can be a big problem and motivates many people to buy mosquito deterrent solutions. Context can also be an important factor. In Northern Europe mosquitoes are only a mild nuisance but in humid, equatorial countries there are lots of hungry mosquitoes some of which carry diseases like malaria and dengue.

Big, frequent problems - problems that happen each day, week, or month - are the best for building a business on. Tied for second place are big, infrequent problems and small, frequent problems. The former are likely to be high value problems and the latter will generate small but regular revenue. Avoid small, infrequent problems. No profitable business can be built on small, infrequent problems. In your customer discovery you'll find no real motivation among customers to solve small, infrequent problems even if you thought it was a big deal, making it a moot point.

Customer Pains & Gains

To grasp the complete picture of the customer's journey to getting the job done imagine filming a mini-documentary of the customer journey.

PAINS

What problems do they encounter preventing them from getting the job done? Are any obstacles or barriers preventing them from accessing solutions? Do they experience usability issues with solutions they are currently using or have used in the past? Are there outcomes they fear and really want to avoid?

GAINS

What do they appreciate in other solutions they have used? What experiences do they talk glowingly about? How do they define "quality"? What makes them smile when getting the job done. These gains may have little to do with the solution itself and everything to do with the interaction with the business after the sale.

Cookie Monsters

Evangelists, earlyvangelists, enthusiasts, visionaries - they go by many names; we like the term cookie monster. Because everyone knows what Cookie Monster loves. Right, cookies! Cookie monsters experience the problem, are searching for a solution and have either hacked a solution themselves or are using a commercial solution. The fact that they are going to these lengths to solve the job shows that it's a big enough problem for them.

A mistake many novice founders make is defining the mainstream market as the customer and trying to create a solution that meets everyone's needs. To paraphrase the poet John Lydgate, "You can please some of the people all of the time, but you can't please all the people all of the time." Your job as a start-up founder is to create something a few customers, cookie monsters, love. Scaling up a business that a small group of customers love is a lot easier than scaling up a business that a large group of customers merely like. Start-ups don't succeed by marketing to the mainstream. Mainstream customers won't take a leap of faith with you and will demand fully-featured solution. They won't even consider your rudimentary minimum viable product. Cookie monsters will.

The early market is the proving ground where the disciplined start-up founder needs to woo and delight customers. If you can't sell to cookie monsters you won't make any sales; at all. But a) there are few of them (maybe only 1% of the market, and b) they don't wear a t-shirt advertising their status.

Problem-Solution Fit

Reading glasses were invented in the 13th century but until the invention of the printing press hundreds of years later they were just a novel idea - they didn't serve a problem far sighted people had. The Blackberry succeeded in the early smart phone market because it focused on solving a single critical functional job:

COOKIE MONSTER RADAR
5 SIGNS TO LOOK FOR

Cookie monsters are willing to adopt new things just for the sake of being the first to try them out. They are the ones that will spend hours struggling to get something to work. They will forgive awful documentation, poor performance, and lack of functionality. They make great critics because they truly care. As customer's, cookie monsters pose fewer requirements than other mainstream customers but they want the truth – and no tricks.

Cookie monster's who love your product become evangelists of your product. They spread the word, recommend you to friends, family, and colleagues and influence buyers and decision makers. ∎

1 EXPERIENCES THE PROBLEM
You know you're talking to a cookie monster because their eyes will light up when talking about the problem.

2 HAS SEARCHED FOR A SOLUTION
You know you're talking to a cookie monster because they'll tell you they're searching for (better) solutions to help them get the job done.

3 HAS USED AN EXISTING PRODUCT
(OR HACKED ONE FOR THEMSELF)You know you're talking to a cookie monster because they'll tell you about the solution(s) they're already using and tried.

4 IS OKAY WITH A BUGGY PRODUCT
You know you're talking to a cookie monster because when you tell them about your solution or give them the MVP they'll be excited about this unpolished thing.

5 HAS A BUDGET
You know you're talking to a cookie monster because they will shift budget or get extra budget just to pay you.

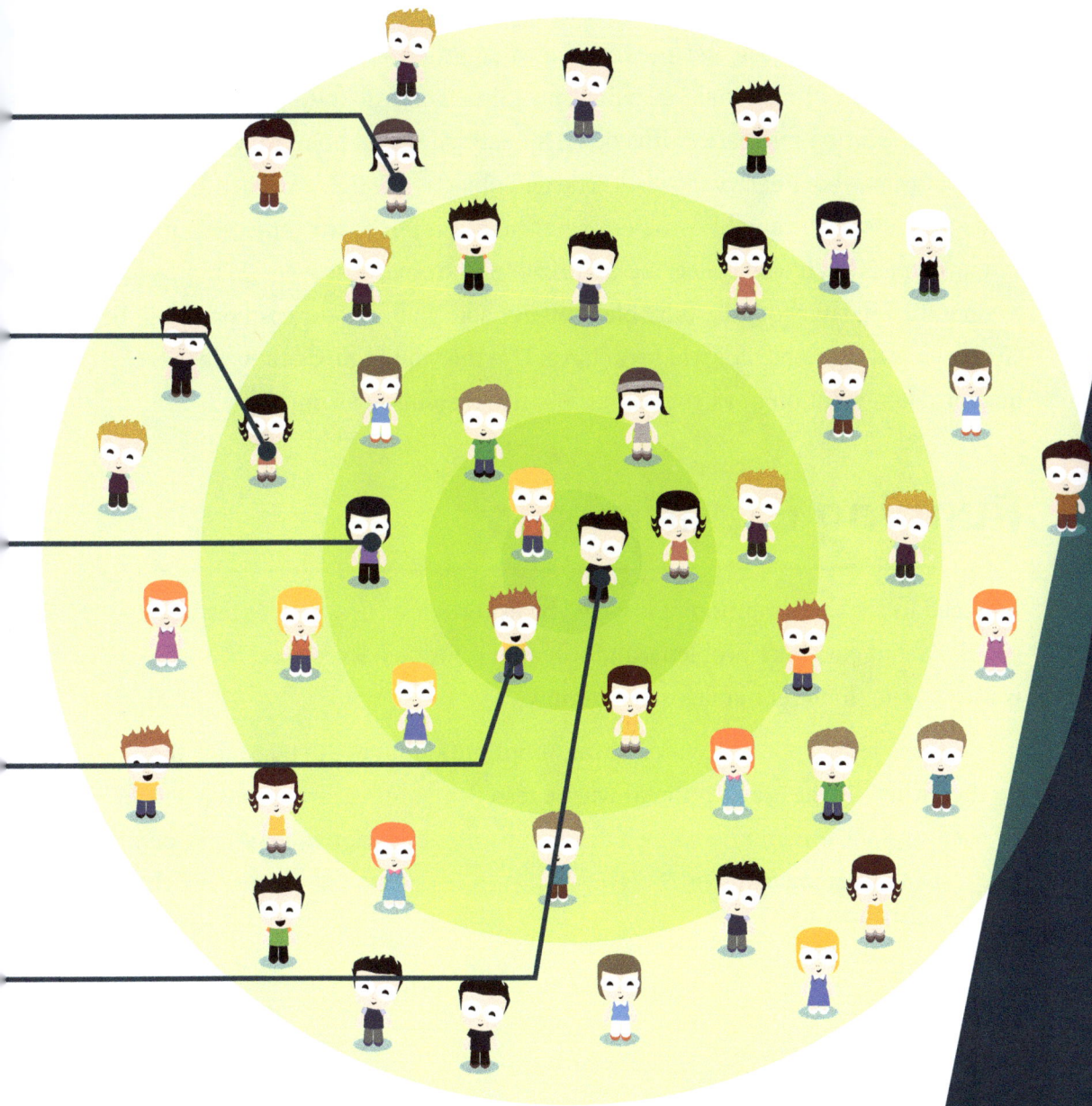

keeping in touch through secure email.

Problem-solution fit is achieved when you've proven the existence of a customer problem and have designed and tested a value proposition that addresses the customers' critical functional job, pains and gains. You will know this for certain when your solution resonates with cookie monsters. At that point they will become your fans, your earlyvangelists. The end objective of the customer discovery phase is achieving a valuable problem-solution fit. In the board game Monopoly when you pass begin you collect a cash prize. In customer discovery do not pass begin until you have found a valuable problem-solution fit. Your cash prize will be customers asking to pay for what you have. Use the value proposition canvas to map problem-solution fit as you test problem and solution asumptions.

Running Experiments

The road to problem-solution fit is paved by experiments designed to test your guesses about customer problems and valuable solutions. Experiments are the way a start-up founder manages uncertainty.

An experiment explicitly defines the assumption(s) that are to be tested, the method whereby the assumption(s) will be tested, what measure of success will be used, and the level for deciding if and when an assumption is right or wrong Use test and learning cards in *Tools for Working* to design and capture insights from experiments.

Pivot or Persevere

After an experiment has been run you will decide what to do based on the result. You have three possible decisions and courses of action. You can pivot, you can persevere or you can iterate. A pivot is a structural course correction, a substantive change of direction. Pivot when your experiments disprove assumption(s) indicating that you are on the wrong trail. Persevere if the experiment validates your guesses and you feel secure about the insights. When an experiment is inconclusive then you must consider the third course of action; iterate. Adjust the experiment and run it again.

Eight pivots

1. **Customer job-to-be-done:** same customer segment, different job-to-be-done.

2. **Customer pains and gains:** same customer job-to-be-done but targeting a different pain to relieve or gain to create.

3. **Customer segment:** same job-to-be-done different segment e.g. from enterprise to consumer.

4. **Channel:** same problem, same solution, different sales and distribution channels.

5. **Revenue stream:** change the way revenue is generated.

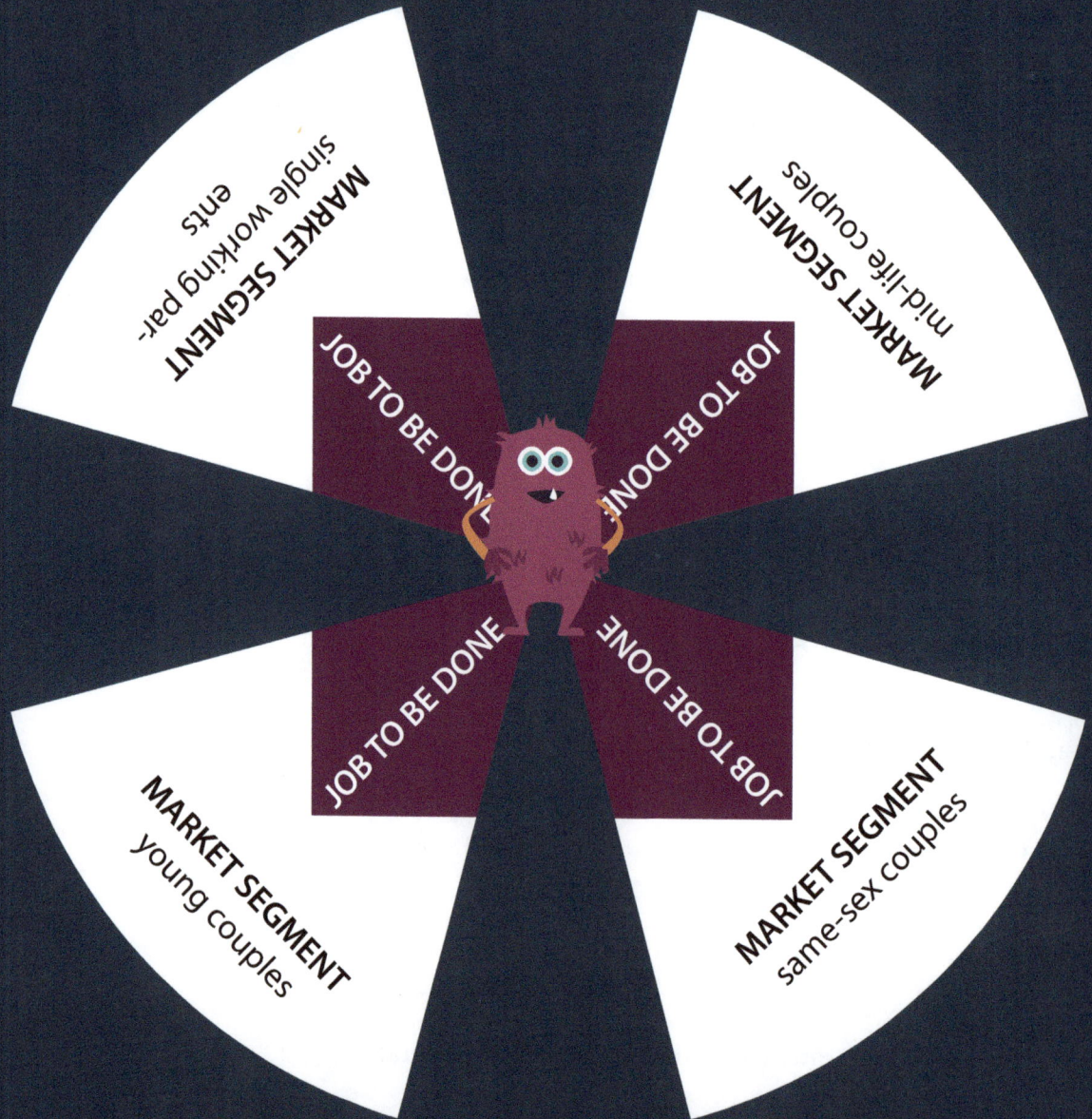

JOB TO BE DONE

MARKET SEGMENT
single working par-
ents

MARKET SEGMENT
mid-life couples

MARKET SEGMENT
young couples

MARKET SEGMENT
same-sex couples

6. **Zoom-in feature:** remove features to focus on just one key feature.

7. **Zoom-out feature:** add features to become more of a holistic solution addressing more pains and gains.

8. **Technology:** solve same job with different technology e.g. wind or solar.

Market Segment Bowling

The market is that whole expanse of people you are interested in serving. It's really going to help your customer discovery to *pre*-segment the market; list groups of people within the market based on some characteristics you believe are significant. For example, the market of parents with infants can be broken down into smaller market segments such as single working mothers/fathers, young double-income couples, same-sex couples, and mid-life couples. A market segment is not the same as a customer segment. Market segments are quickly defined using demographic or geographic criteria. A customer segment is defined by a customer job-to-be-done. Thus a customer segment may be comprised of people from several market segments.

Inventing market segments a priori has several advantages and one big disadvantage. By listing smaller market segments your search becomes much more focused. When you are unsuccessful in finding cookie monsters in one market segment you can move on to the next, and the next, and the next, that is go bowling. When you do uncover a cookie monster in a market segment you have more chance of dominating that market segment. Last but not least you get a roadmap for a marketing strategy. Aftrer successfully dominating a first market segment you have an idea of which to target next, that is go bowling. The disadvantage of listing segments a priori is that you may be completely wrong. Always keep in mind that any market segmentation you do is nothing more than another guess regarding 'significant' contextualisers that needs to be tested.

The alternative to pre-segmenting, continuing the example above, is talking to a lot of parents with infants, of all walks of life. Many, many more.

An important characteristic of a segment, is that the people within a market segment communicate with one another. For example, young parent couples are more likely to be connected with other young parent couples than mid-life couples. When these customers love your product, they will recommend you to others in the market segment but not necessarily across the customer segment. Once you've figured out an important job-to-be-done focus your efforts on bringing a solution to the cookie monsters in a single market segment.

False Positives and Negatives

The two mistakes you are likely to make in customer problem discovery are 1) unwittingly speaking to a single segment and concluding your learnings are applicable to everyone, 2) unwittingly speaking to people from several segments getting conflicting results and concluding it's not a problem for anyone. The first is a false positive, the latter is a false negative.

Suppose you are looking at the general problem of last mile delivery of packages to the home. You know you've got to translate this general problem to a real customer problem. Let's make up some market segments based on the living context.

Urbanites live in the city centre, live close together, many in apartment complexes, have weak social ties with neighbours, and work in the city.

Suburbanites live in houses on the outskirts of cities, have moderate social ties with neighbours, commute to jobs in the city and are thus away from home more hours in the day.

Rurals live in small towns or on farmland, have strong social ties with neighbours, and work locally.

Assume for the moment that you are an urbanite. The first mistake is unconsciously only speaking to people who are most like you, other urbanites, to validate the problem. For some reason it doesn't even occur to you to speak with suburbanites and heavens forbid speaking to rurals! After dozens of conversations with other urbanites you come to the false conclusion that all people, irrespective of living context, experience the same problems to the same degree. A false positive. Alternatively, unwittingly talking to a random smattering of people that include urbanites, suburbanites and rurals you learn that for a few it is a problem to varying degrees of intensity and that for others it isn't a problem. If you run an experiment with a hurdle rate of 50% you will quickly and falsely conclude that enough customers don't experience the problem or that the problem only weakly exists among all customers. A false negative.

To avoid false negatives you need to talk with a large cross section so that differences in living contexts come to the surface in your analysis.

4

~ founders to the start line ~

Contents

A Disciplined Founder's Journey   95

Founder Drive   96

Problem Discovery   98

Customer Watering Holes   98

Three Biggest Problem Conversations   102

Problem Validation Conversations   104

Advice Interviews   107

Asking Follow Up Questions   108

What Not To Do in Customer Discovery   110

Zero in on Customer Segment   116

Cookie Monster Profile   119

Clustering Insight Cookie Monster Profile   122

Would you use it?   124

Ideate Applications   124

Painstorm Problem   125

Root Cause Mapping   130

Brainstorm Solutions   136

The Business Model   137

Freshwatch Alternatives   142

Value Proposition   143

Value Proposition Map   148

Design for Delight   152

The Solution   153

Leap-of-Faith Assumptions   158

Planning Experiments   160

Experiment Methods   162

Revenue Streams   168

Pricing   170

Channels   175

Customer Journey   176

Market Size   178

Too Big, Too Small, Just Right   180

Level Up: Product Market Fit   184

A Disciplined Founder's Journey

Kudos to you that you have the courage to undertake a disciplined founder journey. Take a moment to reflect on what a bold step this really is and on the highs and lows that await you. The elation from validating key assumptions and the devastation at having your darlings shredded. Whether starting from an idea or from a problem it is the learning along the journey that increases your chances of success. Your mission of discovery can be summed in five queries:

1. Does this problem truly exist?

2. Do I fully understand all aspects of the problem?

3. Is my customer segment motivated to solve this problem?

4. Is there a more motivated segment?

5. What can I offer them that will delight?

Look for these six founder drive icons; problem 🐞, resource 🔋, segment ◉, product 🖥, vision-cause 🔭, customer pain 🔥 . Dark grey indicates the section is a vital step for the drive path. Light grey suggests the section is of interest.

FOUNDER DRIVE

Which founder drive best describes your reason for starting something?

FOLLOW THE STEPS ON THE CARD MOST APPLICABLE TO YOUR DRIVE.

CUSTOMER PAIN DRIVE

Painstorm problem, 125 » 20 Problem validation conversations, 104 » Problem smoke test, 162 » Cookie monster, 116, 119, 122 » Brainstorm solutions, 136 » Business model, 137 » Design value proposition, 143, 148, 152 » Advice interviews, 107 » Solution smoke tests, 162 » Solution demos, 162 » Solution prototypes, 162 » MVP, 162

RESOURCE DRIVE

Ideate applications, 124 » 10 Three biggest problem conversations in each application, 102 » Zero in on customer, 116 » 20 Problem validation conversations, 104 » Cookie monster, 116, 119, 122 » Brainstorm solutions, 136 » Business model, 137 » Design value proposition, 143, 148, 152 » Advice interviews, 107 » Solution smoke tests, 162 » Solution demos, 162 » Solution prototypes, 162 » MVP, 162

PROBLEM DRIVE

Problem discovery, 98 » 80 Three biggest problem conversations, 102 » Zero in on customer, 116 » 40 Problem validation conversations, 104 » Cookie monster, 116, 119, 122 » Brainstorm solutions, 136 » Business model, 137 » Design value proposition, 143, 148, 152 » Advice interviews, 107 » Solution smoke tests, 162 » Solution demos, 162 » Solution prototypets, 162 » MVP, 162

SEGMENT DRIVE

Problem discovery, 98 » 40 Three biggest problems conversations, 102 » 20 Problem validation conversations, 104 » Cookie monster, 116, 119, 122 » Brainstorm solutions, 136 » Business model, 137 » Design value proposition, 143, 148, 152 » Advice interviews, 107 » Solution smoke tests, 162 » Solution demos, 162 » Solution prototypes, 162 » MVP, 162

PRODUCT DRIVE

Would you use it?, 124 » Solution smoke tests, 162 » Painstorm problem, 125, 130 » 20 Problem validation conversations, 104 » Cookie monster, 116, 119, 122 » Brainstorm solutions, 136 » Business model, 137 » Design value proposition, 143, 148, 152 » Solution smoke tests, 162 » Solution demos, 162 » Solution prototypes, 162 » MVP, 162

VISION CAUSE DRIVE

Problem discovery, 98 » Three biggest problems per stakeholder, 102 » Zero in on customer, 116 » 20 Problem validation conversations, 104 » Cookie monster, 116, 119, 122 » Brainstorm solutions, 136 » Business model, 137 » Design value proposition, 143, 148, 152 » Solution smoke tests, 162 » Solution demos, 162 » Solution prototypes, 162 » MVP, 162

Problem Discovery

Time to go on a safari; a customer problem safari. Cookie monsters don't wear t-shirts to identify themselves. Whether you're talking to stakeholders of a big cause, talking with a specific target market segment, or just scouting for problems the 'three biggest problems you're currently trying to solve' question helps you adopt a beginners mindset. Aim for at least 20 conversations in each market segment to explore problems.

Approaching strangers is going to feel uncomfortable at first. Keep this in mind: first, it's a conversation, you aren't trying to sell them anything. Second, it's a conversation in which you want to talk about them; their problems. Most people like to talk about their problems. Most of your time will be spent listening to their answers and asking follow up questions to help you really understand their experience. Third, the conversations only have to be long enough to help you reach your objective: to scout and explore real problems. If these problems are worth solving is something you can figure out later. Problem discovery starts with a conversation.

Customer Watering Holes

When you go on a safari in Africa the ranger is generally prepared. They know where the animals were the night before and where they are likely to be that morning. They know which watering holes have water and are frequented by animals. In the customer safari you are the ranger. Where are the watering holes your customers are most likely to come to? Is there a specific location either geographic or online that functions as a watering hole for the people you are interested in talking with about the things they most want to get done and the problems they encounter?

FitsU, a nutrition and exercise schedule service aimed at business travellers, visited the lobbies of four star hotels to talk with people that 'looked like they were in town for a business visit'.

City Furnish, a turnkey furniture rental solution, attended dozens of expat meet-ups in Amsterdam, the Hague and Rotterdam.

SoKitch, an open kitchen for people to cook together and make new friends, went online to dating sites and spoke with singles looking to widen their social connections.

Calculatour, a city tour game based on math puzzles, went to the end destinations of guided walking tours in Amsterdam to talk with tourists.

Bulky, an eating and workout schedule service aimed at amateur body builders, went to gyms to talk with their intended customers.

BabyBox, a newborns supplies home delivery service, went to Prenatal and online parent forums to speak with their target customers.

Not all the starters were successful in finding customers at the locations they visited but they all learnt valuable lessons from the conversations they did hold.

WORKING MOMS CASE STUDY
LOOKING FOR TROUBLE

Let's say you're interested in working moms. See what we did there? We used one adjective and one noun to describe a whole group of people. Adding another adjective like single, working moms would narrow the group down further but we're happy with just working moms for now. You talk with twenty working moms to find out what their three biggest problems are and learn;

» They are exhausted all the time.

» They feel guilty about not doing more for their children and their work.

» They feel like they have no time to do anything well.

» They are both proud of themselves and jealous of the stay-at-home moms.

» They compare themselves against stay-at-home moms, who can go to ballet practice and cook dinner.

» They struggle to find time for their relationship with their partner.

Once you've gotten some insights into the job-to-be-done and pains these moms experience consider, a) if you've heard something that sounds significant,

b) if it's something you could feel passionate about solving. If the answer to both is 'yes', do a second round of conversations to validate the problem. Let's say those last two on the list sound like something significant and actionable and something you could be passionate about.

Talking with a further ten working moms on having no time to cook you learn;

» No one can cook dinner because neither they nor their spouse get home early enough.

» Half don't even like to cook.

» They try all sorts of things to get a meal on the table from frozen dinners, fresh pre-packaged meals, cooking in bulk on the weekend, and trying food box delivery services.

Talking to another ten working moms on having no time for partner you learn,

» They struggle to find time for their relationships with their partner because date night has been so inconsistent that they can't keep a steady babysitter.

» They have struggled to find new babysitters that they trust because they aren't comfortable with strangers.

» Their friends hoard their babysitters so that they are available when needed.

» The cost of babysitter agencies is high.

» Asking friends whose kids are now older is inconsistent.

If you're still enthusiastic now is the right time to brainstorm solutions. ∎

Three Biggest Problem Conversations

In this conversation your aim is to learn about problems people are facing and looking to solve. It is important to adopt a beginner's mindset. This requires approaching each conversation without any preconception about customer problems nor ideas about solutions. Even when you experience the problem yourself don't assume that the way you experience things is true for others. To start the conversation simply ask either:

1. "What are the top three problems you face at this moment?"

2. "I believe that these are the top three problems you face related to getting ... done. Would you agree?"

Ask the conversation partner to prioritize the problems in order of pain, mention higher priority problems they face and describe how they solve the problem today.

PROBLEMS WITH TAX RETURNS

The following example is a fictitious scenario of talking to building contractors about their assumed struggle with preparing and submitting annual tax returns. It's near the end of the fiscal year, walking past a building contractor's van as he's taking a lunch break I decide to try hold a quick opportunistic conversation.

YOU:

"Hi, I'm trying to learn about the top problems contractors experience around getting tax returns done, do you maybe have 5 minutes?"

THEM:

"Sure, why not."

YOU:

"Would you rate these three problems I think you face for me? Filling out the tax forms, keeping administration of invoices and costs, and [problem #3]."

THEM:

"Hmm, OK. So, two is a big hassle for me but I never thought of 1 and 3."

YOU:

"Could you tell me about the last time you ran into #2?"

THEM:

"Yeah, that's easy it happened just the other day..."

YOU:

"What other problems do you encounter with taxes you'd rank higher than [problem #2]?"

THEM:

"You know, the thing that always trips me up the most is..."

YOU:

"That's interesting. I never would have thought of that. How did you solve that?"

THEM:

(tells you how he got the job done last year)

After a bit you thank him for the time and insight he's given you, get his business card and move on.

Problem Validation Conversations

Time to go on a safari; a customer problem safari. Cookie monsters don't wear t-shirts to identify themselves to you. With a *specific* customer problem in mind these conversations are aimed to 1) validate it is a problem, and 2) get a deeper understanding of the underlying causes of the problem. Keep a beginner's mind-set. Don't talk like you know about the problem; especially when you experience it yourself! You talking about the problem and asking a series of semi-structured questions to verify your own experience of the problem only confirms your preconceptions and biases - not their experience. Don't put words in peoples' mouth.

The conversation doesn't have to be long. Your objective is to test the existance of the problem and determine if they are a cookie monster. Aim for at least twenty conversations. Be clear what you're interested in talking about with them. Let them know you want to get their views on a problem you are trying to solve (for them). Quickly and clearly describe the problem as you see it. Adding that you're asking because you're investigating a potential business to solve the problem can be useful but if you're not careful the conversation can quickly be about your ideas for a solution and not their problems. So watch out!

YOU:

"Hi, my name's Lacy I'm looking to understand the problems you experience using an accountant when filing your tax return. Do you have 15 minutes to talk with me about recent experiences you may have had with this issue? I'm investigating this in the context of a possible business but don't want to talk about my ideas but would like to learn about what you experience"

You've done your job to invite him to take you on a journey into their world. Now go into listening mode. Encourage further explanation with follow up questions to explore past experiences with them.

YOU:

"Are you satisfied with the service you get?"

THEM:

"Yeah, pretty much, I give him all receipts and invoices in a shoebox and he does the rest."

[Hmm, that seems inefficient, wonder if the accountant is happy with that shoebox administration. I could stop here thinking there's no way this person could want for anything more, or ask a bit further.]

YOU:

"But...?"

THEM:

"Well, I gotta admit sometimes it's a bit pricey. You know, it's like I work 5 hours to pay this guy for one hour of work."

YOU:

"Yeah, that is kind of steep. Have you ever tried something else?"

THEM:

"Well, I used some software before, but it was difficult to keep up to date with putting all invoices and costs into the program. And then my computer had to get replaced and I couldn't install the software on the new computer. So then I asked around for someone who could help me."

[Ah gold! A better solution for him was a DIY solution, but feeding costs and revenue into the program was an administrative burden!]

YOU:

"Uh huh, and what happened then..."

The conversation continues for a few minutes more. You thank him for the time and insight he's given you, get his business card and move on. Notice the following key points:

1. At no time is there mention of ideas for a solution.

2. Probing follow up questions and helpful nudges get much more interesting information.

Advice Interviews

An advice interview is exactly what it sounds like - interviewing a customer to ask their advice on how to solve a specific problem or on the solution you propose. At this stage your value proposition will be no more than a high level concept not a fully worked out mock-up or prototype. That way if the experiment kills your darlings it won't be a crushing blow, it will only sting. They may rip your idea for a solution to shreds - but what doesn't kill you makes you stronger! These conversations are typically longer than problem conversations.

» Reconfirm the job-to-be-done with the customer.

» Pitch a concept value proposition.

> » Ask for their first thoughts.

> » Ask how they would like to see this job solved.

This will include understanding how they work around the problem today, the solutions they are currently using and where these fail to satisfy. Don't be afraid to ask, "if resources were not a constraint what steps would you take to solve your problem?". Viability and feasibility of ideas can be filtered out later, right now asking a problem-holder to brainstorm for you is the best you can do.

If one problem-holder describes a hack to you that another hasn't tried, or suggests solutions, run these by subsequent interviewees to get their reactions. The most important thing to do in these interviews is explore the ideas shared with you by conversation partners, the upsides and the downsides.

End advice interviews with asking, "if I could solve this problem for you, what budget do you have available now that you would allocate to it?". Of course, don't forget to thank them for their time and insights and let them know you'll be getting back to them within the next weeks or months for feedback on a value proposition.

Asking Follow Up Questions

Always follow up with questions even if the first response appears negative.

YOU:

"Hi, I'm investigating a business idea and would like to ask if you experience X as a big problem? Could you rank it for me in how important it is to you to get done?"

THEM:

"Yeah, I have that. I suppose I'd rank it a 5 on a scale of 10."

Of course you will follow up that negative response with:

THEM:

"Thanks! Say, what are other problems do you have that you'd rate a 10?"

Show genuine interest in the person you're talking to. If a friend came back from a world trip or had an accident you'd be asking loads of questions to understand what they experienced and how they felt. Talking to potential customers is no different. When you do get a strong signal on the job-to-be-done or problems make sure to follow up with questions that probe the reasons behind the response and issue, and the context of your conversation partner when the event took place.

> » What's the hardest part about getting X done?
> » Can you tell me about the last time that happened?
> » Why was that hard?
> » What have you done to solve that problem?

WHAT NOT TO DO
IN PROBLEM DISCOVERY

On the opposite page is an example of a conversation that demonstrates what not to do in customer problem discovery conversations. ■

YOU:

"Hi! I've got this great idea for a business, can I run it by you?"

SETTING UP TO ASK THEIR OPINION ON THE IDEA.

THEM:

"Yeah, sure."

YOU:

"So, you know like Pathé Cinema has this unlimited card where you can pay twenty bucks a month and watch as many films as you want? Well, what if you could do that for all independent art house cinemas in your city? With our card you could go see as many films as you want each week. Do you like it? Do you think it's a good idea?"

ALREADY SELLING!!

FISHING FOR COMPLIMENTS

THEM:

"Uuuh..."

SYMPATHY SEEKING! THEY KNOW YOU WANT SOME KIND, REASSURING WORDS.

YOU:

"Don't worry, I can take it. Tell me what you really think."

THEM:

"Well, I'm not sure how many films people would actually want to see a week."

YOU:

"Oh, I don't think you get it. See, you'd also be able to get discount on drinks so it's like a night out, or making your local cinema like your second living room. You know what I mean? And! you could also get special previews of new movies..."

THEM:

"Yeah, that sounds great."

YOU:

"How much <u>would</u> you pay?"

:(ASKING ABOUT
HYPOTHETICAL FUTURE
BEHAVIOUR.

THEM:

"I dunno. The same as the Pathé unlimited card, I guess? What, maybe twenty-five bucks a month?"

ASKING "WOULD YOU" WITH A
NUMBER ISN'T ANY BETTER.

YOU:

"Would you pay maybe €40? That's cheap compared to a film a week with popcorn and drinks AND you'd be supporting local cinemas and culturally relevant films!"

OH DEAR! ADDING "VALUE"
IN SOME KIND OF APPEAL
TO SOCIAL RESPONSIBILITY.

THEM:

"Yeah, that sounds like a reasonable price..."
IGNORING UNENTHUSIASTIC AGREEMENT

MORE HYPOTHETICAL OPINIONS.   YOU:

"Would you subscribe if it also gave you the inside scoop on new film projects in
the country and a mobile app for connecting with other cinephiles?"

                                    1) ASSUMING THEY ARE A
                                    'CINEPHILE' 2) ASSUMING THIS
                       THEM: IS A JOB THEY CARE ABOUT.

"Yeah, that does sound great. I would definitely use that! Will it also be possible
to go get personal recommendations on new films that are coming out?"

                       YOU: OVERLOOKING THE FLUFF
                                   "DEFINITELY" ANSWER &
                  "Absolutely!"   MISTAKING NON-COMMITAL
                                   IDEA SUGGESTIONS FOR REAL
                       THEM: INTEREST.

"When will it be on the market?"

                       YOU:

"Oh, it's only a concept now but I think I can have it on the market before the
summer."

                       THEM:

"Sounds super. I love it. I'd definitely buy that. Keep me in the loop."

                                   NOT IMMEDIATELY GETTING
                                   CONTACT INFORMATION.
                       YOU:

"Great! I will. Thanks for your time! Oh! By the way, do you think other people would like behind-the-scenes tours of local movie productions?"

ASKING THEIR OPINION ABOUT WHAT OTHER PEOPLE WILL AND WON'T LIKE.

THEM:

"Yeah, that sounds like a lot of fun. I'm sure people would love that."

YOU

"Thanks! You know, its been great talking to you."

BEING SATISFIED WITH THE GLOW OF HAVING YOUR IDEAS CONFIRMED.

YOU

JUST ASSUMED THEY ARE A CINEPHILE, NEVER CHECKED!

(back at the office):

"I had an awesone conversation with this cinephile. They said they loved the idea.
I think we've nailed it. This is the big opportunity we've been looking for!"

YOUR TEAM

(a few months later):

"Why are there no customers? You said people loved it, right?"

YOU:

"I don't know. I talked to hundreds of people. I probably missed something. Don't
worry, I'll go talk to more people and we'll get it right next time."

Say, no! to:

» Fishing for compliments.

» Asking about the opinions of other people.

» Asking about future behaviour.

» Noting ideas suggested as a "todo".

» Letting fluffy answers go unprobed.

» Trying to convince.

» Talking a lot.

» What didn't you like about the solutions you've tried?

» What happened then?

» What happened before that?

» Can you explain that a little more?

» Where were you when this happened?

» How did you feel?

» What was the cause?

» How do you solve it now?

» What does it cost you to solve it today in time, money, energy?

» Are there any goals more important to you than [job]?

Zero in on Customer Segment

Whether you are investigating usage applications for a new technology, scouting for customer problems to solve, or talking to the stakeholders of a cause, at some point you're going to have to settle on a group to pursue further. We covered the idea of a customer bowling alley in part 2. By this time you will have talked to several distinct groups and identified several problems worth solving. Now it's decision crunch time.

Gut check the market segments you know about. Create a table adding each market segment as a column. Assign each market segment a value of 1-3 (1 =

low, 3 = high). Multiply the scores together and sort them from highest score to lowest.

Bite Size – how important the job is, how big a problem it is.

Market Size – how many of this type of customer exist.

Accessibility – how easy is it to find, contact and sell customers in this segment.

Passion - how committed you are to solving this.

Personal advantage - what you can do and know that you have some kind of advantage in addressing the problem.

	Segment #1	Segment #2	Segment #3
Bite Size	2	2	3
Market Size	3	3	3
Accessibility	2	3	1
Passion	2	1	1
Advantage	1	1	1
SCORE	**24**	**18**	**9**

Example segment gut ranking

Start testing hypotheses with the highest scoring segment. If you hit a dead end with the first segment you can pivot to the next until you've got something people love and are happy to pay for.

RANKING BITE SIZE

Ranking bite size involves looking at three factors;

1. Is the job important?

2. Is the pain big?

3. Is the gain essential?

Gut check the market segments you know about. Create a table adding each market segment as a column. Assign each market segment a value of 1-3 (1 = low, 3 = high). Multiply the scores together and sort them from highest score to lowest.

   The job is important to the customer to get done when they have searched for a solution and are actively searching for a solution, have used various market

	Segment #1	Segment #2	Segment #3
Job(s)	2	3	2
Pains(s)	3	1	1
Gain(s)	1	1	1
SCORE	6	3	2

Example bite size gut ranking on scale of 0 - 10

solutions or have hacked one for themselves, give you their attention and ask a lot of questions, want to be kept informed about your progress and lastly, they will have budget earmarked for spending on a solution. The job is unimportant to the customer if doing nothing is an option, if the status quo is preferred above looking for a solution, if solutions are classified as nice to have, if there's no "owner" of the problem, if it's hard to get meetings to discuss the problem. The pain is big when they talked agitatedly or emotionally about the obstacles they encounter. The pain is small when they can't remember what the obstacles are or when they show lack of emotion. The gains are essential when they talk enthusiastically about characteristics that they value. The gain is nice to have when they mention it only in an off hand way.

Cookie Monster Profile

Complete a customer profile for each individual you speak with. Describe:

CUSTOMER JOBS TO BE DONE

What functional jobs is your customer trying get done? (E.g. mow the lawn, or write a report, ...)

What social jobs is your customer trying to get done? (E.g. trying to look good, gain power or status, be seen as competent, ...)

What emotional jobs is your customer trying get done? (E.g. aesthetics, feel good, security, proud about a purchase, ...)

What basic needs is your customer trying to satisfy? (E.g. communication, sex, ...)

CUSTOMER PAINS

Next describe the pains, anything that annoys customers before, during, or after getting the job done such as negative emotions, undesired outcomes and risks.

What does your customer find too costly? (E.g. takes a lot of time, costs too much money, requires substantial efforts, ...)

What makes your customer feel bad?(E.g. frustrations, annoyances, things that give them a headache, ...)

How are current solutions under performing for your customer? (E.g. lack of features, performance, malfunctioning, ...)

What are the main barriers and challenges your customer encounters? (E.g. understanding how things work, resistance, ...)

What negative social consequences does your customer encounter or fear? (E.g. loss of face, power, trust, or status, ...)

What risks does your customer fear? (E.g. financial, social, technical risks, or what could go awfully wrong, ...)

What common mistakes does your customer make? (E.g. usage mistakes, ...)

What barriers are keeping your customer from adopting solutions? (E.g. upfront investment costs, learning curve, resistance to change, ...)

CUSTOMER GAINS

Now describe the benefits, the gains, your customer expects, desires or would be delighted by. This includes functional utility, social gains, positive emotions, and cost savings. Include the minimally expected gains and the optimally desired gains. Expected gains are the industry minimum standards. Desired gains are those that make customers smile extra wide when they encounter them.

Which savings would make your customer happy? (E.g. in terms of time, money and effort, ...)

What outcomes does your customer expect and what would go beyond his/her expectations? (E.g. quality level, more of something, less of something, ...)

How do current solutions delight your customer? (E.g. specific features, performance, quality, ...)

What would make your customer's job or life easier? (E.g. flatter learning curve, more services, lower cost of ownership, ...)

What positive social consequences does your customer desire? (E.g. makes them look good, increase in power, status, ...)

How does your customer measure success and failure? (E.g. performance, cost, ...)

What would increase the likelihood of adopting a solution? (E.g. less investments, lower risk, better quality, performance, design, ...)

COOKIE MONSTER
CLUSTERING
INSIGHT

To establish a cookie monster master profile, analyse your data for patterns on jobs, pains and gains that your interviewees cared about strongly. Synthesise the most frequently recurring jobs, pains and gains into a master profile.

Keep note of jobs, pains and gains that are strongly felt but rare. Outliers, by the very definition, will be excluded in your master profile. In keeping a beginner's mindset; outliers can be rare opportunities. ■

1 Display

Pin all your customer profiles to a wall.

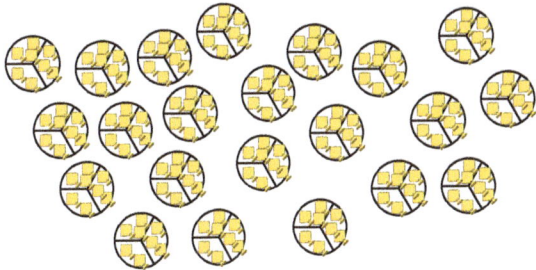

2 Cluster

Group profiles that mention similar jobs, pains and gains.

3 Synthesise 2x

Identify the most common jobs, pains and gains in each cluster. Create a new profile with the most common themes. Now, create a third profile. Can certain themes be expressed more simply, in a single phrase, at a higher level?

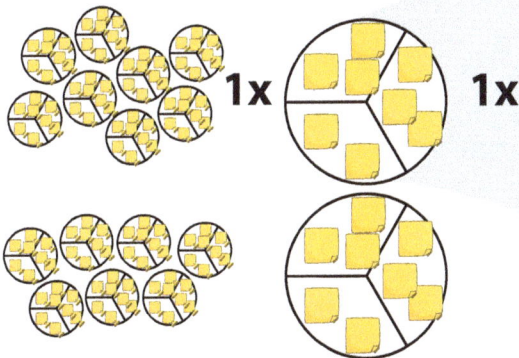

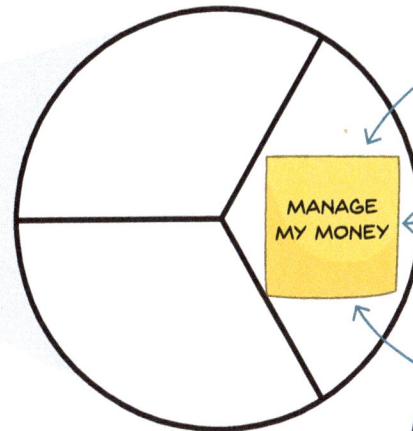

1x

1x

KEEP MONEY SAFE

CHECK AVAILABLE FUNDS

SEND & RECEIVE MONEY

MANAGE MY MONEY

**Synthesis Example:
Banking customer**

Would you use it?

If you've got a grand idea for a product that other people just absolutely can't do without - ask yourself the question, "would I use it?" Novice starters often come up with solutions for "other people". A good example of a frequently occurring "them" solution is mobile personal budgeting applications. Often the starter who conceives the solution struggles with breaking even or saving each month but typically don't use an app to improve their budgeting and for controlling expenses. They may not even have searched for existing solutions or even hacked one for themselves. If you conceive of a solution to a problem you experience yourself, ask yourself, "would I use it? Have I made any effort to solve this before?"

If you do not suffer from the problem, but have conceived a genius solution for others ask yourself "why would they use it?". For example you are not an online retailer but have thought of a dynamite new social retail platform. Why woul they use it? Your hypothetical answers to this question are the assumptions you need to start testing immediately.

Ideate Applications

With a technology or other resource as the drive behind your start brainstorm as many ways in which the technology could be used in different industries. Let's take 3D printing technology (or additive manufacturing as it's more properly called). Can you think of five different ways this technology might be put to use?

Doctors could use it to custom print hip replacements. Engineers could use it to print a bridge. Astronauts could use it to print and recycle the tools they need in space. Kids can use it to print toys. Jet engine manufacturers can use it to print turbine parts. Fashion designers can use it to print clothing. A chef can use it to print a steak. If some of these sounds a little science fiction to you, you're right, they still are. The objective however, was simply to think of possible uses and the users as a starting point for customer discovery.

Painstorm Problem

Rather than brainstorming solutions, painstorm problems. What job is the customer struggling to get done? What is stopping them from achieving their desired outcome? What's the root cause of the problem? Earlier we described using job stories. This is a great tool for painstorming. For example;

I am a home improvement fanatic. When I am in the middle of a new project and want to put the finishing touches on I just can't picture it clearly because I don't have the artistic sensibility. I want to be proud and enjoy the finished project.

Try writing out a few of these to widen your perspective opn what the issues might be.

» continued on pg. 128

SHOPFLOQ CASE STUDY
WHY WOULD THEY USE IT?

Shopfloq was to be a revolution in social commerce. It would empower consumers to form short-term buying collectives, "shop flocks", for products such as furniture, electronics and automobiles. Reatailers, so the thinking went, would love to send collectives an offer in return for higher sales volumes and reduced marketing costs. All they would have to do is offer the shop-flocks a discount which individually, they were unable to negotiate for themselves.

After conducting extensive research into the industry the founders wrote a business plan taking into consideration the reasons earlier similar concepts had failed in the market. The projected sales in the first three years given a modest share of consumption oftargeted product categories was good, the product development roadmap was clear, and development and marketing costs were thoroughly budgetted. The founders had spoken with several early stage angel investors at informal new venture networking events. They had responded with excitement to the idea and had freely brainstormed with them about possible extensions to such a platform. Consumers had tested positively in an internet survey conducted through a professional market research agency.

Deciding to bootstrap the founders built and launched version one of the platform in 2008 with a substantial consumer and business advertising campaign to fuel the growth engine. Only a year later, with no customers and no revenue and a big hole in their bank acounts, the founders decided to pull the plug on the business, cutting their losses. They were left with the question: how could it have gone so wrong?

Despite the extensive market research with consumers indicating a great interest and willingness to use such a social commerce platform the initial spike in sign-ons had seen a slow and inexorable decline when retailer offers failed to materialise. The growth engine quickly stalled - users left and never came back after a first disappointment.

Lessons Learnt

The founders had articulated a "why would they use it" proposition for retailers but had failed to validate the reasoning before building and launching. In post-mortem conversations with the managers at electronics retail stores they learnt that while the promise of greater volumes was attractive retailers were had their marketing promotions budget allocations fixed and were not keen to divert these towards additional discounts. At any rate any such decision would have to be made at the beginning of a budgetting cycle, if it were to be made at all. The idea of giving additional discounts was also something that retailers were hesitant about especially as they expected consumers to be demanding deals on the newest arrivals not last seasons inventory which the retailers were accustomed to discounting. While extra volumes were always welcome, margins on most electronics weren't big, even on the newest televisions. ■

shopfloq™

Social shopping. That's smart.

PAINSTORMING

I am ....

two to three characteristics of customer

When .... *I want to* ....

context   *verb*

but .... *because* ....

pain experienced   *underlying reason(s)*

I want to ....

job to be done

ROOT CAUSE ANALYSIS

Root cause analysis is often mistaken for a quest to identify one main cause. Focusing on a single cause can limit the solutions set, resulting in the exclusion of viable solutions. Root cause analysis is about digging beneath the surface of a problem. The root is a system of causes that reveals all of the different options for solutions.

Root cause analysis is an approach for identifying the underlying causes of an incident so that the most effective solutions can be identified and implemented. It's typically used when something goes badly, but can also be used when something goes well. Within an organization, problem solving, incident investigation, and root cause analysis are all fundamentally connected by three basic questions:

» What's the problem?

» Why did it happen?

» What will be done to prevent it from happening again?

A cause map provides a simple visual explanation of all the causes showing how and why a particular issue occurred. It begins with a few *why* questions (5 whys), then expands into as much detail as necessary (30+ Whys). The cause map creates a visual dialogue showing how all of the pieces fit together to produce a particular incident.

1. Define the issue by its impact to overall goals. People often disagree over how to define the problem. You can get alignment when the problem is defined by

ROOT CAUSE MAPPING
A SYSTEM OF CAUSES

Root cause analysis is about digging beneath the surface of a problem. The root is a system of causes that reveals all of the different options for solutions. Root cause analysis is often mistaken for a quest to identify one main cause. Focusing on a single cause can limit the solutions set, resulting in the exclusion of viable solutions.

It seems that the majority of people find it challenging to positively effect future behaviour and action by actively processing and extracting learning from experiences. Let's apply cause mapping to drill down for reasons why this might be the case.

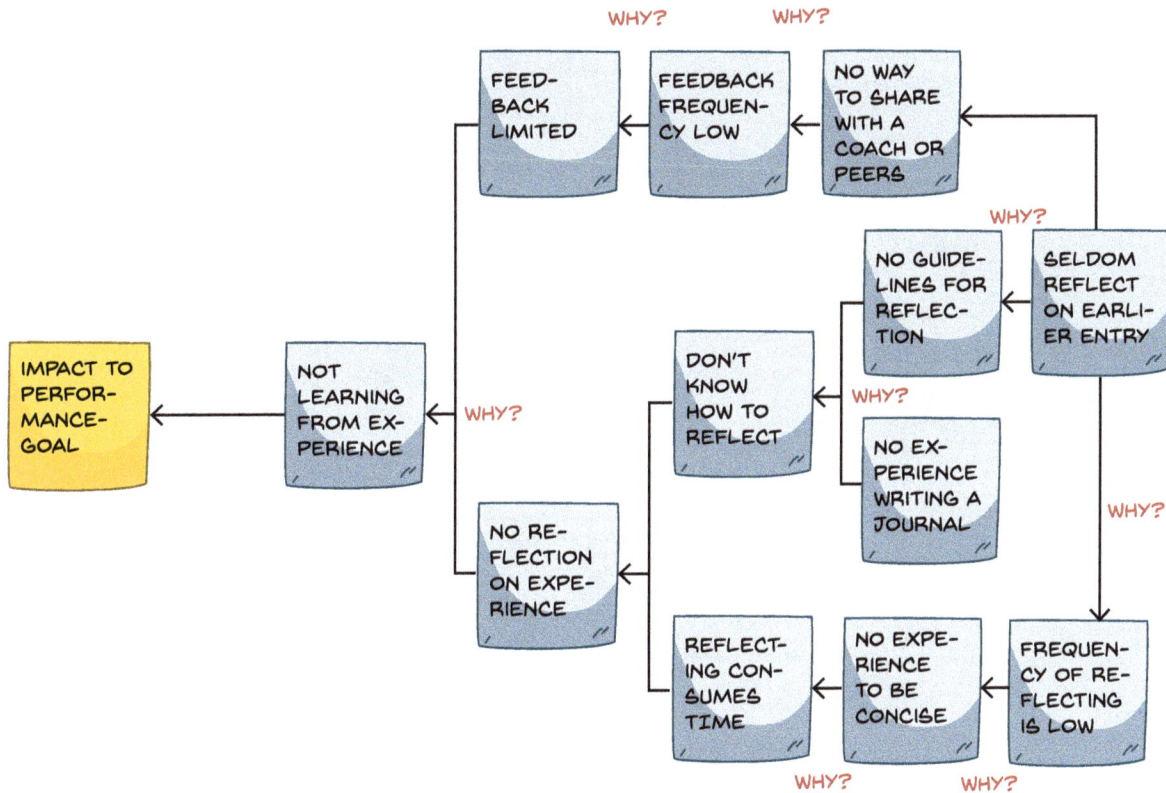

GOOGLE CASE STUDY
FROM CITATION TO WEB SEARCH

In the summer of 1995, Larry Page started as a graduate student at Stanford and began searching for a doctoral thesis topic. It was an important decision as it could frame his entire academic career and found himself attracted to the burgeoning World Wide Web. Page found the web interesting due to the mathematical characteristics. Each computer was a node and each link on a web page was a connection between nodes. A classic graph structure – the largest graph ever created and growing at incredible speed. Many insights awaited discovery and Page set about pondering the link structure of the Web. He noted that while it was trivial to follow links from one page to another, it was nontrivial to discover links back. In other words, when you looked at a web page, you had no idea what pages were linking back to it. He didn't go looking for a better way to search the web, he thought it would be useful to know who was linking to whom.

To understand why he thought it would be useful you need to know about the world of academic publishing. For professors, nothing is as important as getting published; except, perhaps, getting cited. Papers are judged not only on their original thinking, but also on the number of papers they cite, the number of papers that cite them back, and the perceived importance of each citation. Page reasoned that the entire Web was based on the premise of citation – the practice of pointing to other people's work to build up your own – after all, what is a link but a citation?

If he could divine a method to count and qualify each back link on the Web, as Page puts it "the web would become a more valuable place." The original research Page did on such back links he called project BackRub.

At the time the Web comprised an estimated ten million documents, with an untold number of links between them. The computing resources required to crawl such a beast were beyond a student project. Unaware of exactly what he was getting into, Page began building out his crawler. In March 1996 Page pointed his crawler at just one page – his homepage at Stanford – and let it loose. The crawler worked outward from there.

Crawling the entire Web to discover the sum of its links is a major undertaking, but simple crawling was not where BackRub's true innovation lay. Page was aware of ranking in academic publishing, and he theorised that the structure of the Web's graph would reveal not just who was linking to whom, but more critically, the importance of who linked to whom. Inspired by citation analysis, Page realised that a raw count of links to a page would be a useful guide to that page's rank. He also saw that each link needed its own ranking, based on the link count of its originating page. But such an approach creates a difficult and recursive mathematical challenge – you not only have to count a particular page's links, you also have to count the links attached to the links. The math gets complicated.

BackRub's complexity and scale lured Brin a polymath who had jumped from project to project without settling on a thesis. Together, Page and Brin created a ranking system that rewarded links that came from sources that were important and penalised those that did not.

For example, many sites link to IBM.com. Those links might range from a business partner in the technology industry to a teenage programmer in suburban Illinois who just got a ThinkPad for Christmas. To a human observer, the business partner is a more important link in terms of IBM's

≫

place in the world. But how might an algorithm understand that fact?

Page and Brin's breakthrough was to create an algorithm – dubbed PageRank – that took both the number of links into a particular site into account and the number of links into each of the linking sites. This mirrored the rough approach of academic citation counting. It worked.

In the example above, let's assume that only a few sites linked to the teenager's site. Let's further assume the sites that link to the teenagers site also have only a few links. By contrast, thousands of sites link to Intel, and those sites, on average, also have thousands of sites linking to them. PageRank would rank the teen's site as less important than Intel's – at least in relation to IBM.

The long and the short of it was this: more popular sites rose to the top of their annotation list, and less popular sites fell toward the bottom. As they fiddled with the results, Brin and Page realised their data might have implications for Internet search. They noticed that BackRub's results were superior to those from existing search engines like AltaVista and Excite. So far superior that they knew they were onto something big. Since PageRank worked by analysing links, the bigger the Web got the better the engine would get. That inspired them to name their new engine Google, after googol, the term for the numeral 1 followed by 100 zeroes. They released the first version of Google on the Stanford Web site in August 1996 – one year after they met. ■

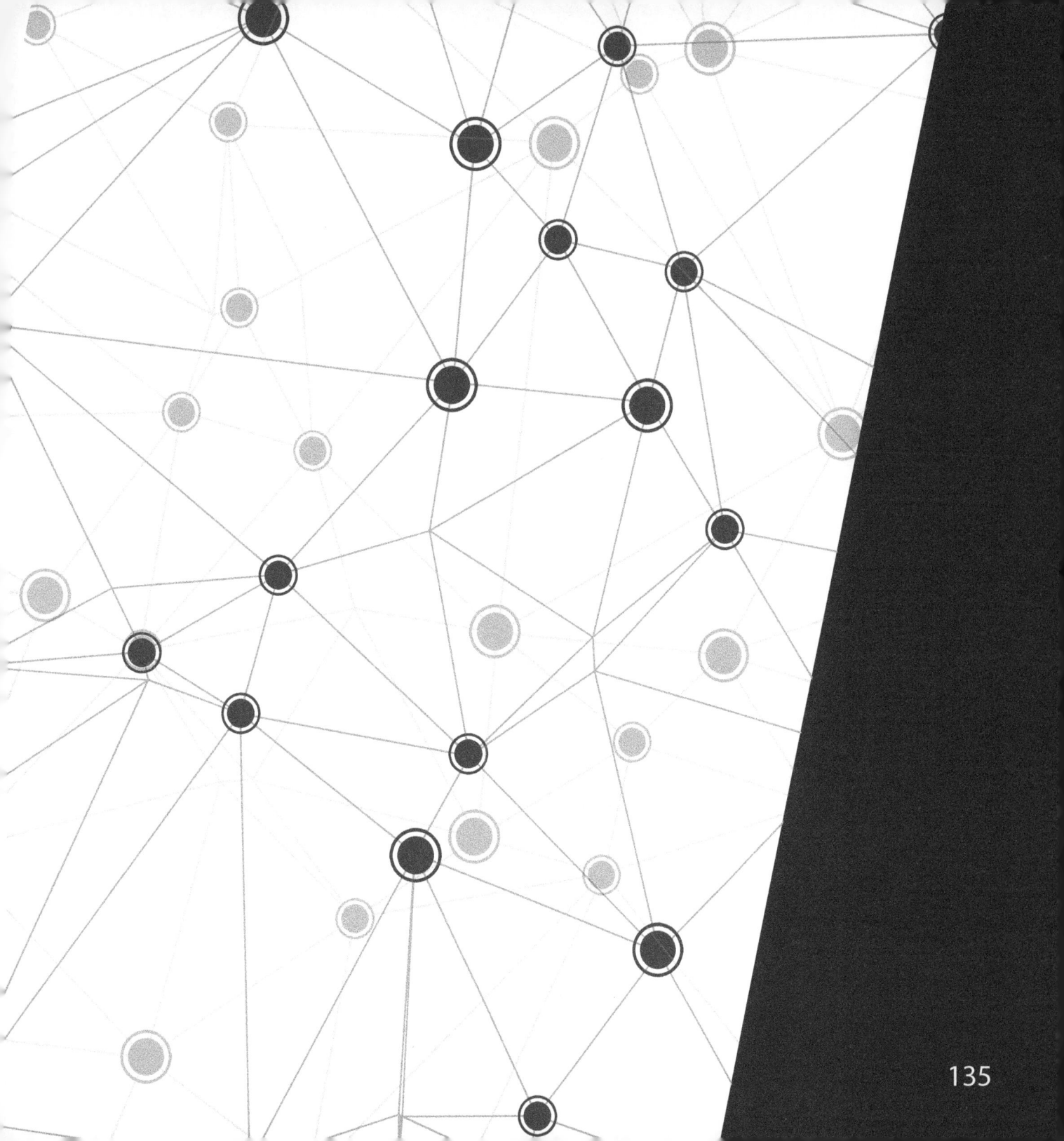

the impact to the goals.

2. Break the problem down into a visual map. Using a cause map provides a thorough explanation revealing all of the causes required to produce the problem.

Brainstorm Solutions

It's time to generate ideas about ways you could solve this. Ask the individuals in your group to write down as many ideas as they can in a given period of time. Have them write each idea or drawing on a sheet or a sticky note. Often, you'll find certain ideas popping up over and over again; in some cases these are the obvious ideas, but in some cases they may provide some revelations. Do a few rounds, each time focusing on a specific customer job or pain as a trigger.

After you've brainstormed you'll need to make some selection and synthesis. Use "dotmocracy" to visualise preferences within the group for ideas. It's a simple and speedy method that avoids the loudest in the room dominating and lengthy discussions. Stick each idea to the wall. Each member gets the same number of dot stickers (post-its will work just as well). Each sticker counts as one vote. Members are invited to place their stickers on the ideas they believe have the most potential. Participants are free to put all their stickers on one idea or to spread their stickers across different ideas. Once the voting is completed, you'll have a visual representation of the group's thinking. Rearrange the ideas so that the ones with the most dots are grouped together and ranked from most dots to least. Talk about the ideas that received the most votes and decide on next steps.

The Business Model

A business model describes the rationale of how an organisation creates, delivers and captures value for itself and customers. The same products, services or technologies can fail or succeed depending on the business model. Exploring different possibilities is critical to finding a successful business model. Settling on first ideas risks the missing potential that can only be discovered by testing different alternatives.

Countless innovative business models are emerging today. Entirely new industries are forming as old ones crumble. Start-ups are challenging the old guard but to be innovative, to be disruptive, to enable underserved customer access to value propositions start-ups must find ways to bring a proposition to market that is 10x cheaper or 10x better. To achieve this you will use existing technology to either create a value proposition or to deliver it to customers (nnless your value proposition is a new revolutionary technology that you intend on licensing to other businesses). Salesforce, for example, used the new world wide web technology of web browsers to deliver software as a service. Netflix used and improved on data compression technologies to deliver streaming video-on-demand services.

REFLECTIVELY CASE STUDY
BUSINESS MODEL PIVOT

The founder of Reflectively, a lecturer in higher education, heard colleagues complain about the same thing over and over - students didn't know how to reflect. Talking casually with them he learnt that the deeper problem was lecturers wanted to help students develop meaningful learning and resilience but the only time they were able to give structural feedback on any reflection was at the very end of a course of study. The current practice was to have students write a reflection report at the end of a ten week period way too late to support meaningful learning. Without direct feedback during the ten weeks the reports tended to be superficial descriptions of what was done, not what was learnt from mistakes, conflicts, meetings, etc. and how the individual adapted behaviour in subsequent similar events.

The problem was the feedback time. Pen and paper made it clunky, email and blogs were messy and separate blogs were either hard to track or couldn't be private if one blog was used. The founder set out to experiment with feedback on reflective writing. First experiments were to ask course participants to maintain a time log of time spent on a course specifying what each log was about. When the course was finished and grades sent students were asked to look at their time logs and comment on what they felt had the biggest impact on their performance. A small handful responded by email.

The next experiment involved the the logbook but now also asked students to set a personal development goal based on a Belbin team role self-assessment and write a paragraph each week on how their behaviours positively or negatively impacted progress on the goal. Each week the logbook and paragraph were handed in and the week after returned with some feedback. This was laborious, inconvenient for both sides, and the feedback still came too late to make much of a difference for students to assimilate and adapt and apply behaviours according to the suggestions given in the feedback. The next experiment built a working digital prototype. It wasn't beuatiful but it had the minimum features needed to work. The response from students was positive in the main regarding the timeliness and usefulness of feedback received, and being conscious of how small behaviours could have a big impact on effectiveness and success.

≫

"A business model describes how a company creates, delivers, and captures value for itself and customers. The same products, services or technologies can fail or succeed depending on the business model."

Alexander Osterwalder

Reflectively™ Software licensing model.

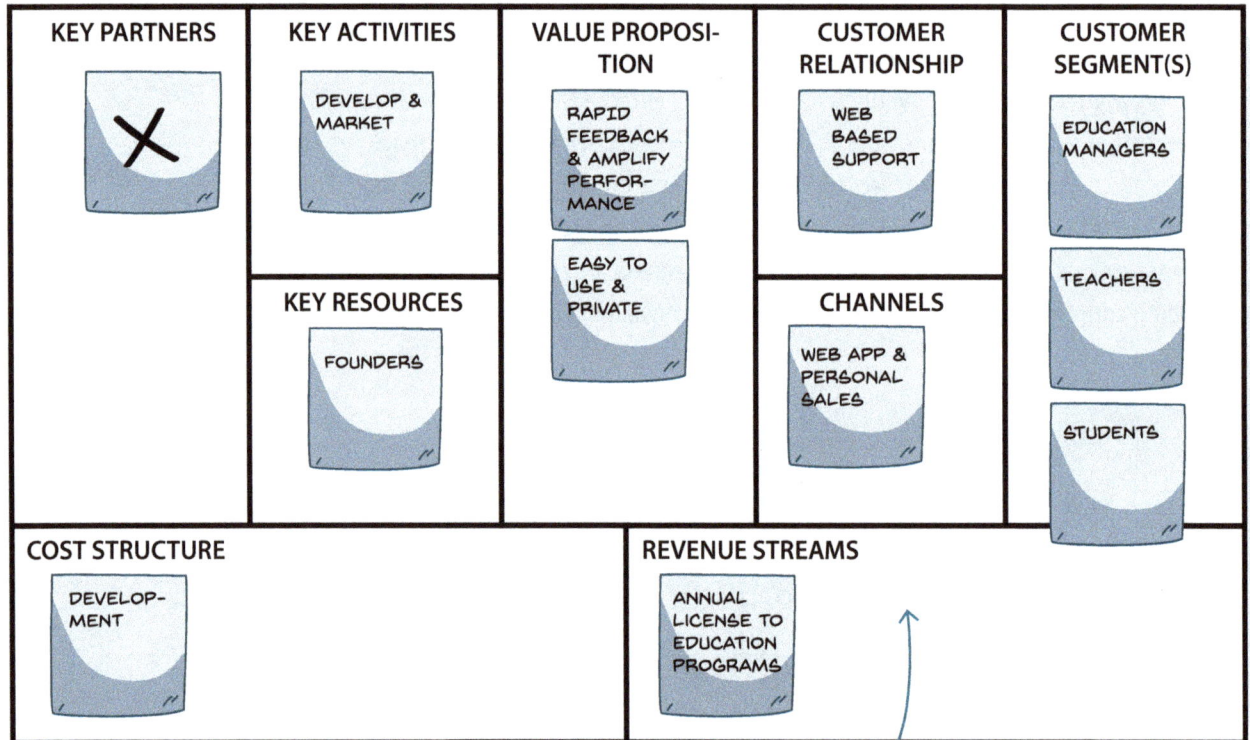

KEY PARTNERS	KEY ACTIVITIES	VALUE PROPOSITION	CUSTOMER RELATIONSHIP	CUSTOMER SEGMENT(S)
✗	DEVELOP & MARKET	RAPID FEEDBACK & AMPLIFY PERFORMANCE	WEB BASED SUPPORT	EDUCATION MANAGERS
	KEY RESOURCES	EASY TO USE & PRIVATE	**CHANNELS**	TEACHERS
	FOUNDERS		WEB APP & PERSONAL SALES	STUDENTS

COST STRUCTURE	REVENUE STREAMS
DEVELOPMENT	ANNUAL LICENSE TO EDUCATION PROGRAMS

First business model hypothesis called for selling an annual license to education program managers (the budget holders), for a fee per student user and an unlimited number of teachers.

⚘ Reflectively™ Fremium subscription model.

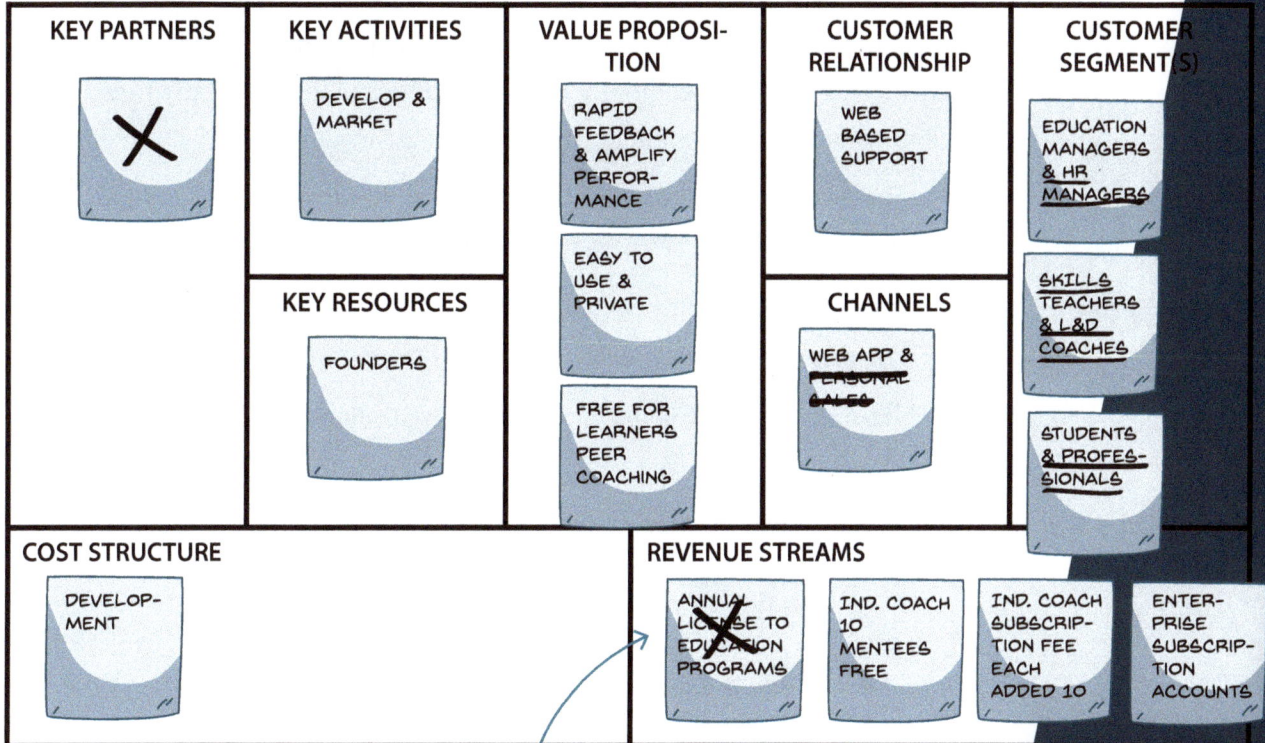

KEY PARTNERS	KEY ACTIVITIES	VALUE PROPOSI-TION	CUSTOMER RELATIONSHIP	CUSTOMER SEGMENT(S)
✗	DEVELOP & MARKET	RAPID FEEDBACK & AMPLIFY PERFOR-MANCE	WEB BASED SUPPORT	EDUCATION MANAGERS & HR MANAGERS

KEY RESOURCES

FOUNDERS

EASY TO USE & PRIVATE

CHANNELS

WEB APP & ~~PERSONAL SALES~~

SKILLS TEACHERS & L&D COACHES

FREE FOR LEARNERS PEER COACHING

STUDENTS & PROFES-SIONALS

COST STRUCTURE

DEVELOP-MENT

REVENUE STREAMS

ANNUAL ✗ LICENSE TO EDUCATION PROGRAMS	IND. COACH 10 MENTEES FREE	IND. COACH SUBSCRIP-TION FEE EACH ADDED 10	ENTER-PRISE SUBSCRIP-TION ACCOUNTS

The revenue stream pivot lead to an open platform free to use for all learners in all walks of life both in education and professionals. Revenue is generated off learning & development coaches who pay a month-ly subscription fee to be able to use the platform to coach mentees. Additionally, enterprise subscription accounts are available for HR and education managers who have 20 or more L&D coaches.

Freshwatch Alternatives

Make a list of three to five alternative offerings. Customers will have talked about these alternatives so you needn't look far to find them. Study the way these create and deliver value for the customer. Ask yourself if they...

> ... produce an attractive cost/benefit? (E.g. in terms of time, money, or efforts, ...)

> ... eliminate risks your customers fear? (E.g. financial, social, technical risks, ...)

> ... limit or eradicate common mistakes customers make? (E.g. usage mistakes, ...)

> ... make your customer's job or life easier? (E.g. flatter learning curve, usability, accessibility, more services, lower cost of ownership, ...)

> ... create positive social consequences that your customer desires? (E.g. makes them look good, produces an increase in power, status, ...)

> ... meets or exceeds something customers are looking for? (E.g. regarding specific features, performance, good quality, good design, guarantees, more of something, less of something, ...)

Select the most important dimensions to customers to compare value propositions against each other. See the case study on *Calculatour* for an example in practice.

Value Proposition

The value proposition states your promise of value to the customer. It articulates what is of greatest value to the customer. In greater detail the value proposition includes the bundle of products & services your value proposition is built around and the specific ways in which you create value for the customer by relieving pains and creating gains (see *Value Proposition Map*).

The proposition can be expressed in a single arresting phrase that focuses your promise to the customer. The phrase is a clear statement of how your product or service solves problems and the tangible benefits customers can expect from using your products or services. Easier, faster, better, less risky, less costly, higher status, exclusive, are value words. Below are some examples from start-ups.

Opera Fast, secure, easy-to-use browser.

Dollar Shave Club A great shave for a few bucks a month. No commitment, no fees, no BS.

FreshBooks Small business accounting software made for you, the non-accountant.

Mint Be good with your money from the big picture to the details that matter.

Look in the back of the book for six templates to help you articulate your value proposition.

CALCULATOUR CASE STUDY
FRESHWATCH ALTERNATIVES

After mapping the value creation dimensions of direct competitors and alternatives the Calculatour team plotted the value they wanted to deliver to customers; an engaging and challenging experience. The value proposition would be as easy to use as joining a guided tour, as convenient (at your own time) as city guide book and apps walking tours and entertaining and challenging like pub quizzes and treasure hunts.

The channel for the value proposition was a mobile application. They figured they could drop the live tour guide altogether and replace this with video and audio content replace and a chatbot that users of the app could pose questions to. They added mental challenge and reasoned the maths couldn't be too hard otherwise people would feel bad, they further added team based competition and personal recognition and reward for achievements. They decided they could make the tour like a treasure hunt game by unlocking next clues and destinations through solving maths problems, and lastly enabling people to customise their urban adventure by designating areas in the city they were interested in exploring to fit within their other activities.

»

Legend:
- Culinary & History Tours
- City Guide Walking Tours
- Mobile App Tour
- Calculatour
- Ingress
- Geo-caching
- Treasure hunt
- Pub quiz

GAINS CREATED BY ALTERNATIVE CITY TOUR SERVICES

GAINS CREATED BY ALTERNATIVE CITY ENTERTAINMENT

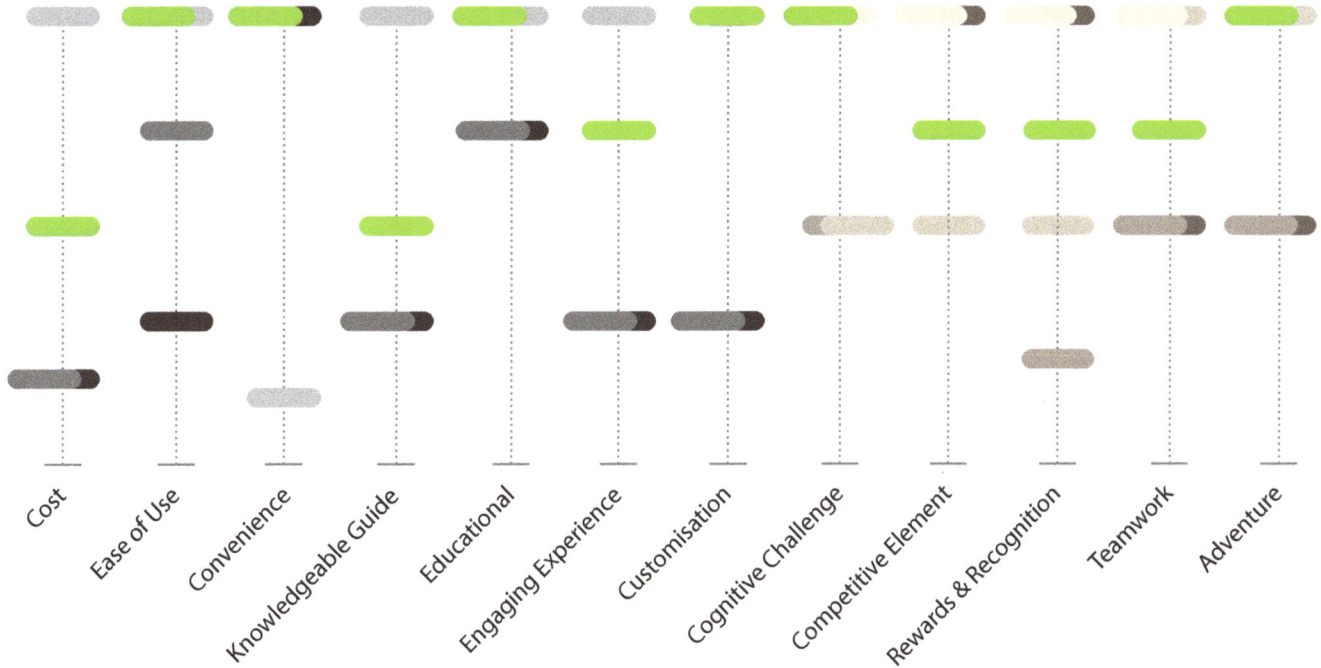

Categories (x-axis): Cost, Ease of Use, Convenience, Knowledgeable Guide, Educational, Engaging Experience, Customisation, Cognitive Challenge, Competitive Element, Rewards & Recognition, Teamwork, Adventure

Boxes:
- TOUR CITY
- FUN TEAM COMPETITION
- LEARN & CHALLENGE
- EXPLORE TOGETHER
- CUSTOMISE TO OWN AGENDA
- EASY TO USE & START ON OWN

After this they then looked at the implications providing all this value would have on the business model. They identified a potential new revenue stream for people participating in citytour (pub) quiz. Calculatour would have to organise such events and this impacted the key activities. They also realised that some form of player question support was required, that would impact customer relationships activities and might call for a user community, for people to post and search for answers from other users in lieu of a human tour guide. It meant possibly making sure an employee was always online to respond to questions if no community users were actually on hand to answer questions.

For providing this value to the customer, for solving the whole customer job, they believed they would be able to ask a fee in line with live guided historical and culinary tours.

a city tour app, identified the free walking routes in city guides, downloadable walking route mobile apps, and historical and culinary guided tours as customer alternatives. They studied what it was that customers of these alternatives valued about the solution and drew up a list of value creators.

Cost General tours aren't that valuable but niche tours customers are willing to pay quite a bit for.

Easy to use Books are relatively easy but apps are even easier and narrate.

Convenience Book routes and apps allow tourists to set their own start time and pace.

Tour guide A live tour guide is appreciated for local knowledge.

Informative Interesting factoids are a definite perk.

Ability to ask questions Conversations with tour guides are appreciated, especially with more niche tours.

They then looked outside the direct tour market at other value propositions and business models related to exploring the city. They came up with a shortlist of the mobile game Ingress, geocaching, treasure hunts, and pub quizzes. Although the latter has little to do with exploring the city they decided to include it in their list because of the fun nature of quizzes while centered on knowledge and trivia. They identified a list of value creators that these offerings provided their users.

Cognitive challenge Solving problems gave a sense of satisfaction.

Competition Competing against other individuals and teams in pub quizzes and Ingres increased the fun.

Teamwork Having others to spar with in pub quizzes made the experience more meaningful.

Rewards & recognition Getting recognised for achievement gave pride of accomplishment.

Adventure The element of the unknown in treasure hunts made it exciting.

Customisable Being able to go on your own schedule was better than locked into someone else's schedule. ∎

Value Proposition Map

Draw out your value proposition in it's entirety describing the bundle of products and services your value proposition is built around and how your products and services alleviate customer pains and create gains.

BUNDLE OF PRODUCTS & SERVICES

The iPod was a superior music player - it was more durable, easier to use, stored more songs, and was aesthetically pleasing. But without iTunes to make creating and syncing play lists it would have solved only a fraction of the real problem. Your proposition may include supporting products to help your customer perform their roles of buyer and decision maker (compare, decide and buy). Your proposition is likely to be composed of various types of products & services:

Physical such as manufactured goods.

Intangible such as copyrights or after-sales assistance.

Digital such as music downloads or online recommendations.

Financial such as insurance or financing.

Now list all the products and services your value proposition is built around. Ask yourself which products and services you offer that help your customer get either a functional, social, or emotional job done, or help him/her satisfy basic needs?

What are the primary features your value proposition must have to help the customer solve the job? Are peripheral or complementary products or services needed?

PAIN RELIEVERS

Now lets outline how your products and services create value. First, describe how your products and services alleviate customer pains. How do they eliminate or reduce negative emotions, undesired costs and situations, and risks your customer experiences or could experience before, during, and after getting the job done?

What characteristics of the value proposition are designed to relieve the customer pains? Does the customer experience current solutions as difficult to use? How will you make it easy to use? A clean and intuitive interface design? Do customers experience current solutions as boring? How will you relieve this boredom? Will you include personalisation in some way? Do customers experience that current solutions break quickly? How will you relieve this pain? By making it from stronger materials or by eliminating moving parts? Explicitly outline how you intend to eliminate or reduce the most important things that annoy your customers before, during or after they are trying to complete the job or that prevent them from accessing solutions. Ask yourself if they...

> ... produce savings? (E.g. in terms of time, money, or efforts, ...)

> ... make your customers feel better? (e.g. kills frustrations, annoyances, things that give them a headache, ...)

> ... fix underperforming solutions? (e.g. new features, better performance, better quality, ...)

... put an end to difficulties and challenges your customers encounter? (e.g. make things easier, helping them get done, eliminate resistance, ...)

... wipe out negative social consequences your customers encounter or fear? (e.g. loss of face, power, trust, or status, ...)

... eliminate risks your customers fear? (e.g. financial, social, technical risks, or what could go awfully wrong, ...)

... limit or eradicate common mistakes customers make? (e.g. usage mistakes, ...)

... get rid of barriers that are keeping your customer from adopting solutions? (e.g. lower or no upfront investment costs, flatter learning curve, less resistance to change, ...)

GAIN CREATORS

Lastly, describe how your products and services create customer gains. How do they create benefits your customer expects, desires or would be surprised by, including functional utility, social gains, positive emotions, and cost savings? What characteristics of the value proposition are designed in to create the gains customer's appreciate in alternatives? Fun? Add a gaming or competitive element. Community? Help them connect with other customers. Integration with other things? Make it connectable. Nice to look at? Then pay attention to design. Outline how you intend to produce outcomes and benefits that your customer (minimally) expects, and desires including functional utility, social gains, positive emotions, and cost savings. Ask yourself if they...

Focused on
EXPERIENCES
People, Activities, & Context

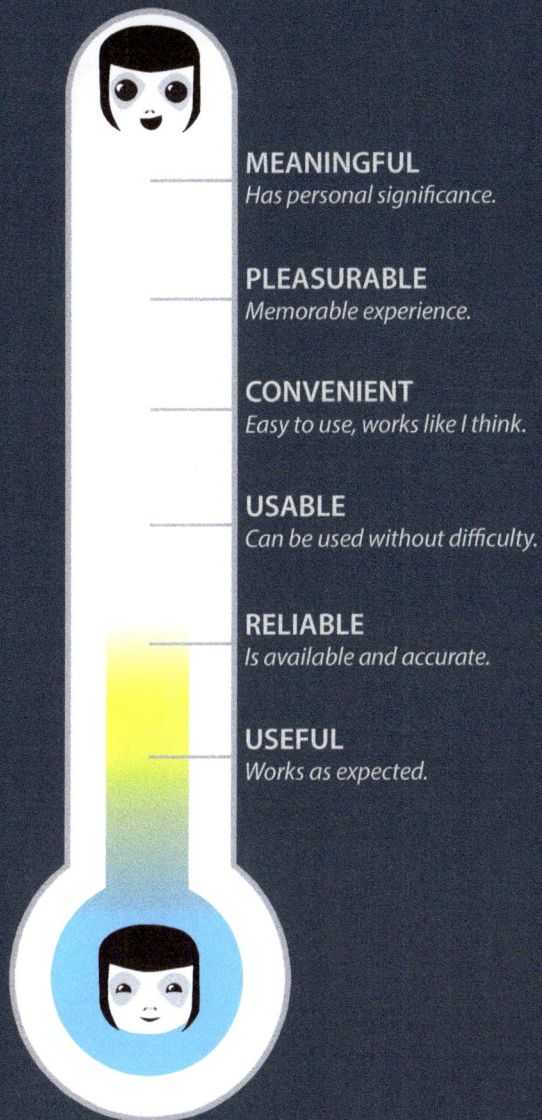

MEANINGFUL
Has personal significance.

PLEASURABLE
Memorable experience.

CONVENIENT
Easy to use, works like I think.

USABLE
Can be used without difficulty.

RELIABLE
Is available and accurate.

USEFUL
Works as expected.

Focused on
FUNCTIONAL JOBS
Products & Features

...create savings that make your customer happy? (e.g. in terms of time, money and effort, ...)

... produce outcomes your customer expects or that go beyond their expectations? (e.g. better quality level, more of something, less of something, ...)

... copy or outperform current solutions that delight your customer? (e.g. regarding specific features, performance, quality, ...)

... make your customer's job or life easier? (e.g. flatter learning curve, usability, accessibility, more services, lower cost of ownership, ...)

... create positive social consequences that your customer desires? (e.g. makes them look good, produces an increase in power, status, ...)

... do something customers are looking for? (e.g. good design, guarantees, specific or more features, ...)

... produce positive outcomes matching your customers success and failure criteria? (e.g. better performance, lower cost, ...)

... help make adoption easier? (e.g. lower cost, less investments, lower risk, better quality, performance, design, ...)

Design for Delight

Your MVP must solve the critical functional job at the very least. Serving attendant emotional or social jobs is also important for creating an experience as is

creating the gains sought and relieving annoyances. But a product experience isn't limited to using the product. It is also the customer's interactions with the business.

Each interaction the customer has with your product and business, each touchpoint on the customer journey from awareness, to buying, to receiving and consuming and getting help, is an opportunity to create a delighting experience. Apple's retail stores are a good example of creating a delighting experience around buying, accepting (delivery), and getting help. But stores like these aren't cheap to maintain. Coolblue the online retailer tries to make it's e-commerce sites very easy to use, payment even easier, and it's delivery and installation services a joy. Communication, sales, distribution and customer relation channels are vital in this respect to pay attention to; creating awareness, helping customers evaluate the value proposition, enabling purchasing of the value proposition, delivery of the value proposition, and after-sales support.

The Solution

The solution is the value proposition plus the bundle of products and services (features) plus the customer experience. For example, the iPod's value proposition is to effortlessly play and carry hundreds of music tracks with you. The bundle of products and services which the value proposition is built around are the iPod player itself, the iTunes software, the iTunes store, and firewire. The customer experience is an elegant user interface, automagic synchronisation between laptop and iPod when connected, and software that is quick to respond.

CLUBETEN CASE STUDY
A DINNER PARTY LIKE MOM'S

Clubeten started out mass market - all fraternity and sorority student clubs needed their service: a box of food to prepare their weekly dinner together. The founder, a member of a fraternity club, experienced the issue himself. Very quickly into customer discovery he discovered that most fraternity clubs were perfectly happy with the same spaghetti each week but sorority clubs were different. Sorority clubs wanted to put on a dinner party quality meal that didn't break the limited budget and wasn't difficult or time consuming to prepare. Each week a different sister would be "on duty" and many were terrified at the prospect of letting down the others - of repeating what someone else had done, of preparing a tasteless or otherwise boring meal.

Clubeten put together it's first MVP; a box with ingredients that included Google Maps-like cooking instructions linked to a step-by-step video they had made and uploaded to YouTube. They included a bottle of Prosecco and candles to give the meal that "dinner party" sparkle, paid particular attention to the box itself in order that unpacking it would be festive and made delivery personable.

»

Value proposition A box of dinner ingredients for student club dinners.

Customer All student clubs have a weekly dinner together but dislike shopping. The customer job is functional to get the ingredients and prepare a meal. The only pain is keeping within budget.

Value proposition A box of dinner ingredients for sorority clubs changing each week.

Customer Sorority clubs find it important to have a cozy, special dinner. Fraternity clubs don't expereince any problem with just spaghetti or pizza each week.

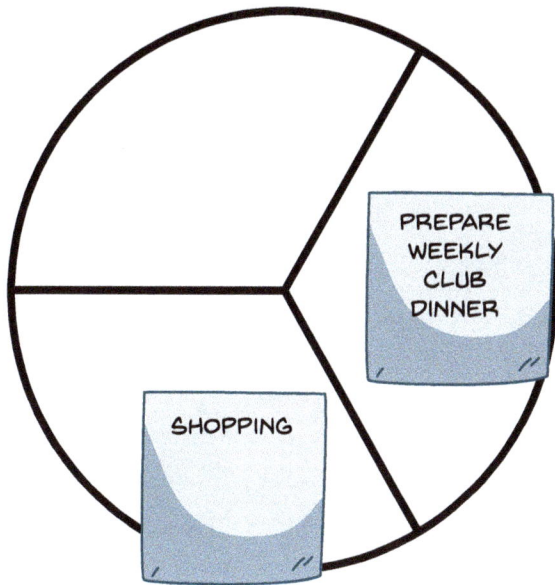

PREPARE WEEKLY CLUB DINNER

SHOPPING

SORORITY CLUB WEEKLY DINNER

FEEL COZY

SHOPPING

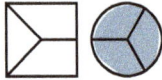

Value proposition undefined.

Customer Sororotity clubs actually enjoy doing the shopping as a social event but lack creative cooking skills. They want to avoid duplicating earlier dinners and want to create a festive dinner for sorority sisters.

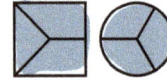

Customer Sorority clubs experience shopping as a bonding moment. Lacking creative cooking skills they are mortified to let their sisters down with either a duplicated dinner or lack luster event. They strive to create a festive dinner for each other.

Value proposition Dinner party like mom puts on. Meals history, send suggestions for next dinner, send a festive box of ingredients that will be an adventure to unpack together. Included are necessary condiments and navigation-like video cooking instructions, a bottle of Prosecco and candles.

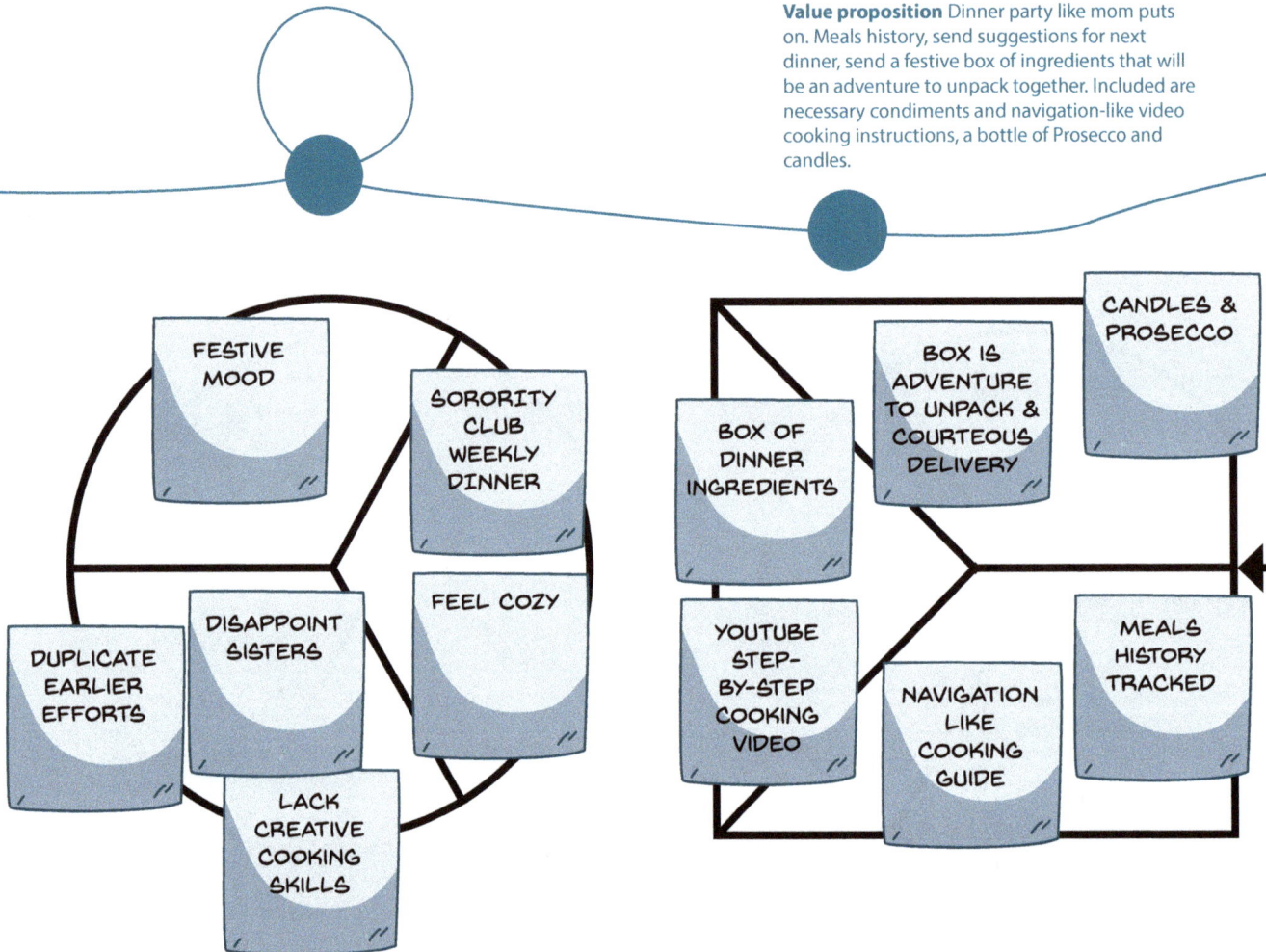

FESTIVE MOOD

SORORITY CLUB WEEKLY DINNER

FEEL COZY

DISAPPOINT SISTERS

DUPLICATE EARLIER EFFORTS

LACK CREATIVE COOKING SKILLS

BOX OF DINNER INGREDIENTS

BOX IS ADVENTURE TO UNPACK & COURTEOUS DELIVERY

CANDLES & PROSECCO

YOUTUBE STEP-BY-STEP COOKING VIDEO

NAVIGATION LIKE COOKING GUIDE

MEALS HISTORY TRACKED

These elements were essential to the sellable MVP as they addressed the main job and delivered on the value proposition 'a dinner party like your mom used to put on', created excitement in customers and spread the word.

They paid attention to tracking the first ten boxes delivered and the recipes used. They followed up with the sorority clubs after the dinner to learn what they loved about the service and how they could improve. Everything was done manually. Recipe instructions were printed on normal paper and videos were shot by the founder, the boxes were generic costing 25 cents and stamped by hand for branding. The founder went shopping at various supermarkets in his neighbourhood to find the best products at the lowest cost and packed and delivered the boxes himself. ■

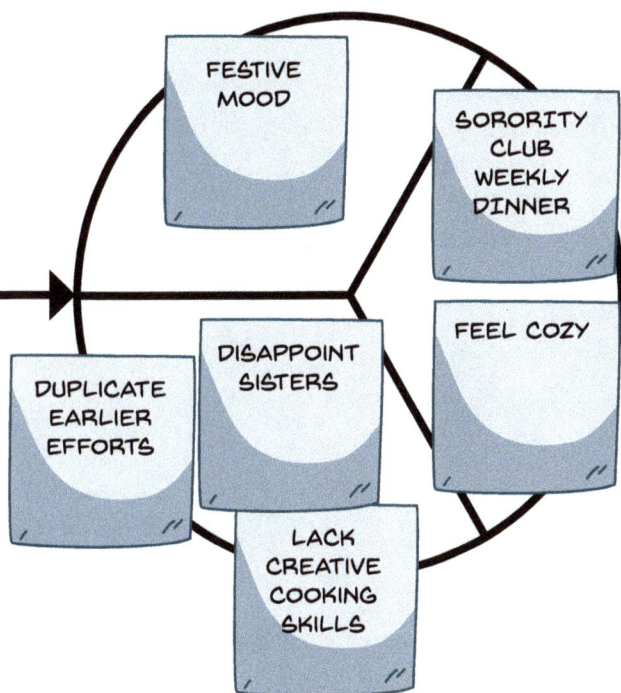

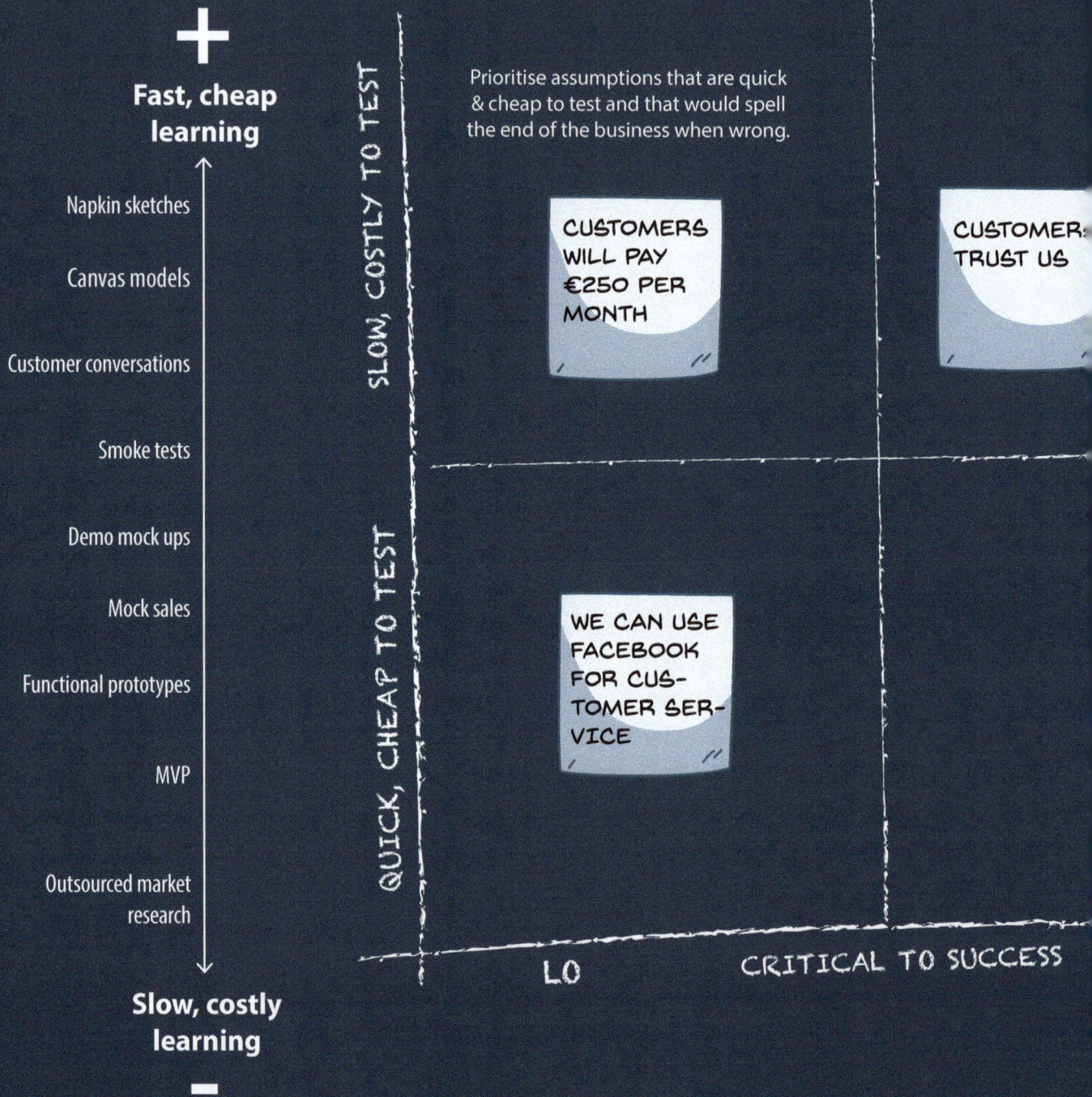

Leap-of-Faith Assumptions

Cramming too many assumptions into one test will make it difficult to distinguish what you are testing and accurately observe the outcome. What are the most risky assumptions about your customer jobs, pains, gains, bundle of products and services, pain relievers, gain creators, revenue streams, and channels?

» How critical is the assumption to the success of the business - when you are wrong it could spell the end?

» How quickly, easily and cheaply can you test the assumption?

HI

PLANNING EXPERIMENTS
DISCIPLNE & TRANSPARENCY

Develop a test cards for the riskiest assumptions. Those that are a) most critical to the business success and b) easiest and cheapest to test in the shortest amount of time. The faster you can test assumoptions the greater your *learning velocity*, the faster you will separate fact from fiction and the faster you will be able to build a product that customers are wildly enthusiastic about. Ask the questions you are afraid to ask - kill your darlings or you will learn another kind of lesson!

TEST CARD

TEST CARD

We believe that...
[Customer segment] wants to [job to be done] and wants to avoid [unwanted outcome].

HYPOTHESIS

To verify this we will...   RISK HIGH MEDIUM LOW
Talk with 50 people we believe to be within the customer segment, face-to-face.

TEST METHOD

And measure...   RELIABILITY HIGH MEDIUM LOW
Recognition of [job], AND Recognition of [unwanted outcome], AND the emotional response to both.

METRICS

We are right when...
30 of the 50 recognise both the [job] and the [unwanted outcome] and show a strong emotional response.

SUCCESS CRITERIA

Date march 22   HURDLE HIGH MEDIUM LOW

Who Robert

1 Backlog
Place the most important tests on the Experiment Board.

VALIDATED   INVALIDATED   UNDEFINED

TEST CARD   TEST CARD

TEST CARD   TEST CARD

TEST CARD

TEST CARD   TEST CARD

LEARNING CARD   LEARNING CARD   LEARNING CARD

TEST CARD

3 Extract learnings
Review if the assumptions in an experiment are validated, invalidated or undetermined. Pivot, persevere, or iterate.

TEST CARD   TEST CARD

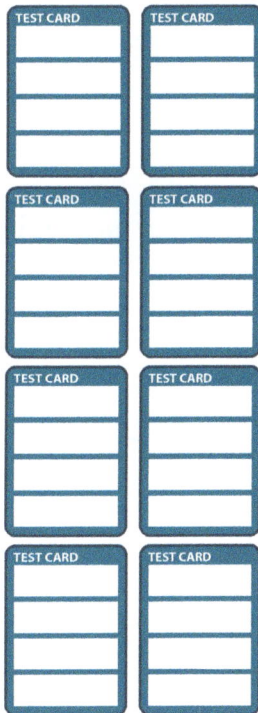

2 Build & run experiment
Select test cards to run next. Build the test method and start running the experiment.

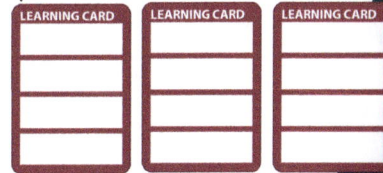

Experiment Methods

You can use your imagination to think *how* you can test assumptions. In the following pages we've described some of the more common methods that have evolved in the start-up world.

CONVERSATION

You can test your assumptions most cheaply (with the exception of your own time), through holding a conversations.

SMOKE TEST

Smoke tests can be anything that tries to get feedback from a customer on a problem or a value proposition and encourages them to get in contact with you rather

MINIMAL VIABLE PRODUCT   WIZARD OF OZ   CONCIERGE   U

PROTOTYPE

than you looking for people to engage in conversation.

- » An advert in the news paper with a phone number.
- » A poster with a phone number, web address, or email address.
- » A web landing page with a signup form.
- » A Google Adwords campaign leading to a landing page.
- » Postcards left in cafes with a QR code, phone number, or email address.

Smoke test slogans are designed to either test the problem or the proposition. If you've got the right problem or the right value proposition cookie monsters will respond enthusiastically to your smoke test. They'll gladly give you their email address, phone number or some other piece of value in exchange for being kept informed.

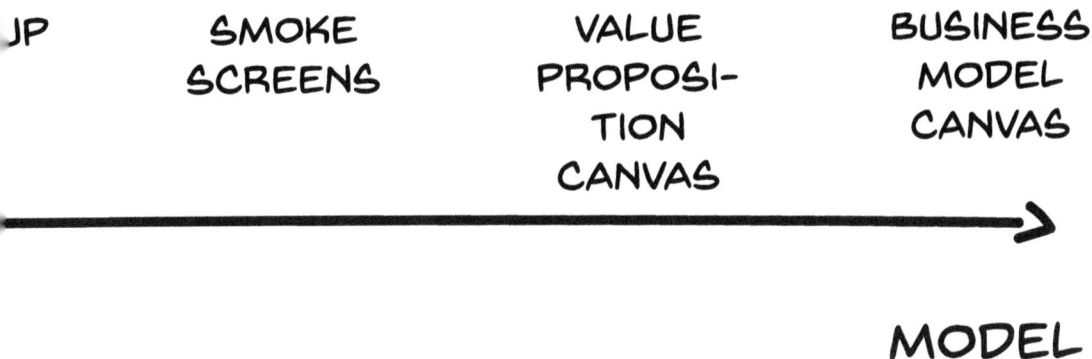

JP   SMOKE SCREENS   VALUE PROPOSI- TION CANVAS   BUSINESS MODEL CANVAS

MODEL

DEMONSTRATION MODEL

Demonstration models are like smoke tests but require a little more effort. Anything that demonstrates how your solution relieves pains and creates gains while getting the job done can be a demonstration model. In the aerospace industry a clay model (or computer simulation) is used in very early design phases to test the airflow over the fuselage and wings. Models aren't the real thing. in some form models simulate the proposition.

For example;

» a value proposition canvas model.

» a business model canvas of the business.

» a storyboard illustrating a customer scenario and your imagined value proposition.

» a brochure or an online video telling the problem and how the customer solves it using your value proposition.

» physical product box with user instruction booklet.

» a clickable application wireframe.

The line between a model and a prototype may in some cases be very thin. Contemporary innovation practioners use the words interchangeably and often treat the concepts as interchangeable too. It is, however, for practical purposes, better to draw the line somewhere. Models are useful for testing aspects of the product before building a prototype. They are faster and cheaper to build. As tests methods go, models have proven as useful to lean start-up entrepreneurs as clay models (or computer simulations) are to aeroplane designers. Models help test non-product stuff – like advertising channels and value propositions – early in the development process. Alexander Osterwalder supplied business strategists with a *model* in the Business Model Canvas: a model of how the business does or could work. Later work in value proposition design introduced the *prototyping* of value propositions using the value proposition canvas. Nevertheless, keeping a strict definition of prototyping and remaining consistent with business modelling this is an incorrect usage of the term. It would be better to speak of value proposition *modelling*.

Use your imagination to simulate your value proposition for customers with a minimum of effort and cost.

PROTOTYPE

The X-1, an experimental supersonic jet, is what many people think of first when prototypes are mentioned. Something about these daring pilots and cutting edge aerospace designs just capture our imaginations. It's not surprising to find that dictionary definitions cite jet plane prototypes as use examples. A prototype in the aerospace industry is the first full-scale and usually functional form of a new type or design of a plane. To learn about necessary changes, engineers have to test the design under real flight conditions. In this use, prototypes occur quite late in the development process.

Human centered design (thinking) practitioners were building prototypes long before the lean start-up movement. In the early days when design thinking was still about physical objects, practitioners mocked up prototypes of products using materials at hand. Some prototypes were simple mockups while others actually worked. Apple's original mouse is a trusty example of building a fast prototype using a butter dish, a deodorant roller ball and basic electronics.

Building a prototype – even a plain one – requires some technical expertise and resources. Building a prototype when a model will do wastes resources. Building a model when a prototype is needed will get you no insight.

CONCIERGE

Concierge is a non-technical prototype in which the value proposition is created and delivered manually to a single customer, live, step-by-step to understand how the solution meets the needs of the customer each step of the way. Concierge prototypes are well suited services-type businesses.

WIZARD OF OZ / MECHANICAL TURK

From 1770 until its destruction by fire in 1854 The Turk, an automaton, constructed and unveiled in 1770 by Wolfgang von Kempelen, appeared to be able to play a strong game of chess against a human opponent, as well as perform the knight's tour, a puzzle that requires the player to move a knight to occupy every square of a chessboard exactly once.

The Turk was in fact a mechanical illusion that allowed a human chess master hiding inside to operate the machine. With a skilled operator, the Turk won most of the games played during its demonstrations around Europe and the Americas for nearly 84 years.

The wizard of Oz in the book The Wonderful Wizard of Oz, was believed to be an all powerful being until revealed by Dorothy, the main protagonist, to be a man operating a illusion making machine.

Wizard of Oz and Mechanical Turk are today synonyms for a class of prototypes that are non-technical functioning service prototypes. *Aardvark* a social search service start-up launched in early 2008, connected users live with friends or friends-of-friends who were able to answer their questions, also known as a knowledge market. Users submitted questions via the *Aardvark* website, email or instant messenger and Aardvark automagically identified and facilitated a live chat or email conversation with one or more topic experts in the 'askers' extended social network. Only, when *Aardvark* launched it's first prototype, there was nothing automagical about it. The *Aardvark* founders manually sent the questions to people themselves using IM and email and then manually replied to the user through the *Aardvark* website. When first launched, *Aardvark* was like the Mechanical Turk, user's didn't know it was being done by hidden human hands. It meant the founders could test their service proposition cheaply and quickly requiring no expensive application development.

MVP

The MVP (minimum viable product) is the smallest thing you can build that delivers customer value and gets you paid. The MVP is different from an advanced prototype in that it actually delivers the value proposition. The MVP lacks many features that may prove essential later on. However, creating an MVP does require quite some extra work. We must be able to measure it's impact with customers and test the growth hypothesis - how new customers will discover a product and subsequent adoption/ usage.

MOCK SALES

Sell a product in one location only (either physical or online), for a limited time. As a bonus, you can even try out different prices!

Revenue Streams

The revenue stream is the way in which you generate revenue off a customer. What method of paying would be most convenient for the customer and represents the thing that they truly value? When iTunes first launched they continued the music industry revenue model - selling ownership to a copy of a song (not to be confused with licensing copyrights). Baby boomers and to some extent generation X valued ownership and attached longer term value to a song. In return for the ownership of a digital file of music and the right to play the song as much as they wanted each customer paid a fixed sum of money i.e. a (digital) asset sale was made.

Millenials and Generation Z is different in the relation of the individual to music. With a hundredfold increase in contemporary artists and music available - not to forget the immense library of a centuty of recorded songs, music albums (what an archaic idea) and individual tracks have less lasting value. Generation Z are less interested in owning music to put in a collection and are more interested

Nine Common Revenue Patterns

Asset Sale	Transfers ownership of a physical product from one party to another, eg. groceries.
Subscription	Charged (monthly) for continuous access to service, eg.mobile telephony.
Rental	Temporarily granting access to an asset for a fixed period of time, eg. a vehicle.
Leasing	Granting exclusive, long term access but not ownership to an asset, eg. an apartment.
Licensing	Giving permission to use protected intellectual property or an asset, eg. a brand.
Commission	Received for brokering between two or more parties, eg. an auction.
Usage	Charging a rate per unit of consumption, eg. electricity.
Advertising	Space provided to promote a product, service or brand, eg. billboards and adwords.
Sponsorship	A sum of money provided for association with a brand, person, organisation or activity.

in having access anywhere, on any device. Spotify fills this need with a streaming music service, first advertising supported and later offering subscriptions.

Changing the revenue stream mechanism can form an innovation in itself making a product more accessible or more affordable for customers. Automobiles have been around for over a hundred years and that has enabled smart entrepreneurs to figure out different business models and revenue streams based on cars. You can buy a car, new or used. When you buy a car you can either pay for it in full or take a loan from the car dealer, paying in installments and paying interest on the remaining principle. You can rent a car either through a rental agency or through a peer-to-peer platform. By signing a short-term contract you have the use of a specific car for the determined (usually short), period. You can lease a car. Leasing is similar to renting except that leasing is generally for a long period of time and garauntees exclusive use to a specific car. You can subscribe to a shared car service like Greenwheels. For a fixed subscription fee per month you can access any car in the Greenwheels fleet and drive anywhere. Lastly, you can take a taxi and pay a usage fee per kilometer or minute (Uber works the same as far as revenue stream is concerned).

Pricing

Pricing becomes very relevant when launching an MVP. Without a price you can't capture value. Of course, you might try A/B tests to test a range of prices but that's out of the scope of this book. iTunes priced a single song at ninety-nine cents. A single song on Spotify is more like a commodity, it has almost nil value.

For €9,99 a month a subscriber can listen to as much music as they want. If you listen to only one song a month that song costs €9,99. If you listen to the same song a hundred times a month that song costs nine cents. If you listen to thousands of songs in a month the price per song drops to almost zero. Pricing expresses a measure of value to the customer. We can see from the above example that generation Z doesn't value a digital asset like a music file. The value is in the access; anywhere, anytime, any device. There are three ways to come to a pricing estimate;

1. Benchmark the pricing of current solutions used.

2. Estimate the internal cost to the customer of achieving the job to be done.

3. Determine the value that a customer places on having the thing of value.

BENCHMARKING

Pick three competitive and alternative solutions to benchmark a price range. Establish a price point at the lower end, the mid-range and the upper limit. Experimenting with price bracketing when you present your MVP to your customer can help determine a real value pricing for later.

CUSTOMER INTERNAL COST

You can mirror the cost of alternatives but that doesn't really tell you what the value you can create for the customer. You want to disrupt the existing market meaning making it accessible for underserved customers too, right? What does it cost underserved customers in terms of money, time, or stress to solve the job?

Suppose a rough estimate shows it costs the customer €100 to currently solve the job (not the cost of a competitor solution but the actual cost of labour and materials). You could charge €100. But suppose that creating and delivering a proposition will only cost you €30. Do you;

a. charge €100 making a big profit?

b. charge €40 covering your total costs and making a very modest profit?

c. charge €65, splitting the value?

Your aim is to capture value for the customer and yourself. You could capture all the value yourself and be very happy but that wouldn't leave the customer really excited about your innovative solution - it may be easier to use, better in quality, etc. but at the end of day it doesn't improve their bottom line result. You could charge the cost price plus a small markup and make the customer really happy with a massive saving but that doesn't really represent the value of your offering and you need to make a decent profit too, not just scrape by.

A win-win can be created by splitting the €70 difference fifty-fifty with the customer. A price of €65 will delight the customer with a solution that solves their job better than the current alternative and they save money. And you can be happy with a healthy gross profit margin and a have made a fan out of the the customer.

VALUE TO CUSTOMER

Early solution tests may quantify value through non-monetary exchanges such as a pre-order or booking without actually paying. You're going to have to come up with a hypothesis of what solving this job is worth to the customer. Here are some ways to think about arriving at a reasoned hypothesis. Quantifying a value proposition involves three steps:

» List the (business) outcomes your solution impacts (e.g., improvement in the percentage of just-in-time deliveries).

» Select a customer metric that will demonstrate the impact of the business outcome (e.g., reduction in inventory x annual inventory carrying costs = value of just-in-time deliveries).

» Determine the most compelling anchor for bringing the metric to life (e.g., compare the outcome of your solution against the status quo or compare it against your estimate of the competitor's solution or against other companies in the customer's market space).

PRICING DEATH FOR STARTUPS

The first mistake when pricing is using a cost plus method as described in scenario B 'Customer Internal Cost'. This under prices innovative solutions as it fails to account for value created for the customer. A retailer on the other hand, generally adds little value other than access to product, and therefore it is appropriate that they use a cost plus margin pricing approach. As an innovative new solution your value added is greater. But how much greater?

The second mistake when pricing is believing the price has to be less than competitors. When entering an existing market with many competitors, a red ocean, a commodity product is unlikely to succeed against competitors who have been in the game longer and already optimised their business model to compete at cost. As a start-up, you do not have the power to undercut prices as your cost per unit will be higher with your fledgling business. Focus efforts on innovating on the industry's standard business model understanding where you can still add value which incumbents are unable or unwilling to deliver and price accordingly.

Channels

Channels come in many types, especially in the digital age; communication channels, sales channels and distribution channels. Pre 1980's the world was simpler for marketers. Sales and distribution channels were all physical, with the one exception of telesales. Today, there are physical sales channels for physical products, physical sales channels for digital products, digital sales channels for physical products, and digital sales channels for digital products. Some sales channels are also distribution channels, and mnay digital platform services are their own sales and distribution channel.

For example, buying music (itself an anachonism I'll admit), you used to go to a physical retail store and buy a physical medium first vinyl records, then tape cassettes and later compact disks (which technically speaking brought in the digital era). Buying a physical carrier of music has moved to downloading single tracks or albums on iTunes and other digital channels, and even mopre recently downloading is displaced by streaming music using a service like Spotify. The song - a unit of music - unchanged, but the sales and distribution channels have

Digital Bytes	Physical Bits
Own website, webshop, tele-sales, or software-as-a-service (delivery of a service through the web browser, eg. software, films, coaching)	Retailers and dealerships
E-commerce platform such as Amazon, iTunes, and Alibaba	Wholesalers and distributors
Social commerce sites like Facebook, Groupon	Direct mail sales catalogue
Auction sites like eBay	Sales force
App stores like Apple Store, and Google Play Store	Package delivery services & vans
Industry aggregators like Independer, and Skyscanner	Value added reseller
	OEM or systems integrator

Digital and Physical Sales & Distribution Channels

CUSTOMER JOURNEY
IT'S NOT JUST THE PRODUCT

Many jobs take several steps to achieve the goal. Hiring a self-study course to learn new skills includes the steps researching and selecting one course out of many and applying the new found skills later. Customer job journeys come in all shapes and sizes; the well known visualisation of a day-in-the-life, or the map of interactions a customer has with the channels of a business offering impling an existing existing sales and distribution channels used by the business.

Customer jobs theory suggests looking at what a customer does before, during and after getting a job done to understand the experience, progress and context of the customer and reveal the customer's problems, anxieties, pains, aspirations, expectations and delights. Don't get hung up on a specific method but rather use what seems appropriate to your specific challenge. Imagine you are creating a documentary about your customer. You can ask things to build the picture, you can observe, you can include what's historically significant and what's happening in the moment. Decide what makes sense.

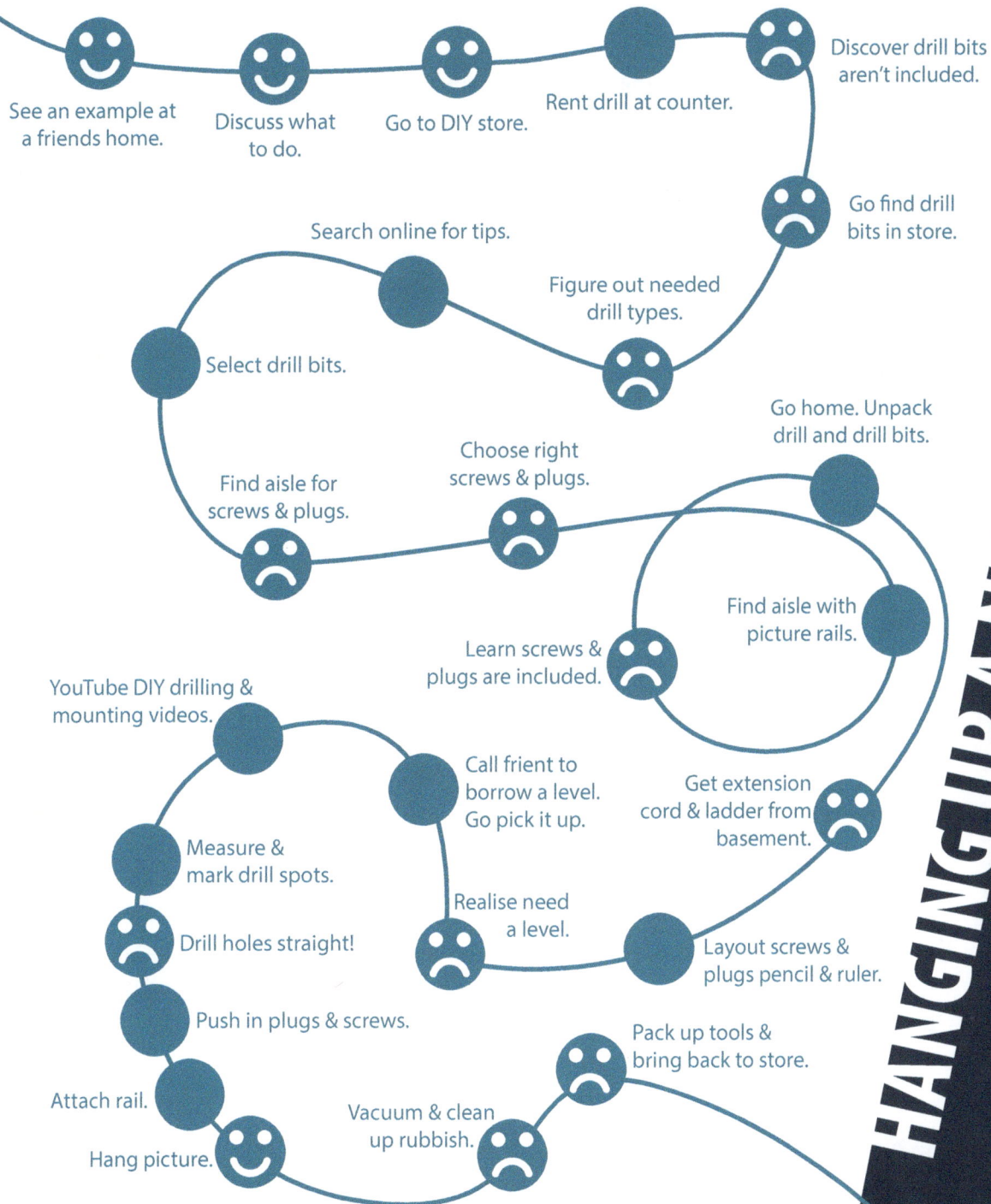

See an example at
a friends home.

Discuss what
to do.

Go to DIY store.

Rent drill at counter.

Discover drill bits
aren't included.

Go find drill
bits in store.

Search online for tips.

Figure out needed
drill types.

Select drill bits.

Go home. Unpack
drill and drill bits.

Choose right
screws & plugs.

Find aisle for
screws & plugs.

Find aisle with
picture rails.

Learn screws &
plugs are included.

YouTube DIY drilling &
mounting videos.

Call frient to
borrow a level.
Go pick it up.

Get extension
cord & ladder from
basement.

Measure &
mark drill spots.

Drill holes straight!

Realise need
a level.

Layout screws &
plugs pencil & ruler.

Push in plugs & screws.

Attach rail.

Pack up tools &
bring back to store.

Hang picture.

Vacuum & clean
up rubbish.

changed significantly, making consuming music more accessible, at a lower cost and anywhere. iTunes and Spotify didn't innovate music, they created innovative business models by changing the channels whereby music is consumed.

Communication channels, for nurturing customer relationships, have also seen a lot of innovative activity that enabled smarter business models. Not only dedicated mobile apps but also social media pages on Facebook and groups on LinkedIn, Twitter and others have vastly expanded the marketers ability and responsibility to engage customers in dialogue. Communication can be one-size-fits all such as FAQs on a website, Instant Messaging with a chatbot or person, email contact, facebook and twitter support accounts, a telephone helpline, online customer accounts such as banks and insurers offer that enable customer self-service, customer communities where customers answer each other's questions or share information, and also personal account managers. The communication channel and customer relationship deeply influences the overall customer experience and can mean the difference between success with a mediocre value proposition and failure with a great value proposition.

Market Size

'Is this market segment big enough to build a business on?' is a question that every founder must consider regularly during customer discovery. The TAM (total available market) is in this respect the most important back-of-the-envelope calculation you can make. It is a estimate of the real number of customers in the segment and the frequency with which they buy. Such a 'bottom-up' approach to

market sizing is more difficult to perform due to estimating real customers than a traditional marketing 'top down' approach using demographic statistics, but will lead to a better, more realistic estimate. Try and count the heads (literally) of potential customers in a small sample. For parents with children under ten wanting to enjoy a date-night once per month, it would be possible to do a headcount of parents at primary schools in a region to arrive at a rough TAM. Suppose I estimate the total market in my city at a hundred thousand parents who on average go out once a month.

Next, I will want to have some idea of the serviceable available market (SAM). This is the number of customers I could reach and serve with my available resources and communication, sales and distribution channels in the first year. Some of the parents in my area may have family such as grandparents living near by who can babysit for an evening. A survey amoung parents can help surface this type of information and arrive at a more accurate SAM of parents experiencing irregular date nights. The ability to actually serve the SAM is limited by availability of babysitters and babysitter's travel limitations but we'll leave this out of consideration for now. With my own website being my sole sales channel how many of the parents with no family in the region regularly search the internet for a babysitting service (they may have alternatives such as hiring a neighbours' daughter to sit for them from time to time). Knowing online search analytics on words such as 'babysitter tonight' I calculate I can reach maximally five thousand customers in my city. Does the market look big enough to you?

Before answering that, consider the SOM (serviceable

The minimum viable segment is a segment you can dominate and that is big enough to fuel your growth.

obtainable market). The SOM is that number of customers that actually buys multiplied by the frequency of buying. Knowing that prospect-to-sales conversion rates on websites are typically low at around 2,5%, I estimate that my SOM will be about one hundred and twenty-five customers in the first year usng the service on average once per month. Therefore, I know that I can maximally expect to sell 1,500 babysitting services in my first year. Does the market look big enough to you?

The cookie monsters of your market will be the first to adopt your new innovative value proposition. You may find cookie monsters in several market segments that together form a customer segment defined by the customer jobs-to-be-done but will need to focus on one market segment to begin with. The first market customer can be thought of as the MVS (minimum viable segment). This is a segment you can dominate with your limited resources and reach. That means having the cookie monsters rally to your banner to attract and convince the late majority (mainstream) within that segment. Market leadership in your MVS is valuable to your positioning and credibility for the next segment you want to go after (see Market Segment Bowling). Once you have won the whole market segment, you can claim leadership and consider expending your value proposition to the cookie monsters in the next market segment.

Too Big, Too Small, Just Right

Is the segment too big is perhaps the better question to ask. The ability to own the segment is equally as important as the potential. Like Goldilocks, you want your segment to be 'just right'; not too big, and not too small. There is no objective measure or rule of "too big" or "too small" just as there is no objective measure of a mountain that is too big or too small to climb. This depends on the abilities of the climber and the rewards desired. For founders, 'too big' a segment can only be measured in relation to the resources they can muster - or are willing to muster - in a short span of time, and their experience. When a segment is too big, you will struggle to win a majority of the customers before competitors join and if you can't reach more than 10% of customers with your channels and resources within two years, you may end up being not the great white shark but merely a tiger shark in your own blue ocean.

'Too big' may also be in relation of who else will be attracted to the market. If the TAM is a billion in revenue, this might attract many larger competitors, hungry to fuel their growth. Large competitors have a resource advantage while you have a nimbleness advantage. It's not a foregone conclusion who will win, but it's worth thinking about before taking the giant on. Too big or too small is different for start-ups and large established companies. A segment that is worth a million in revenue will solicit a yawn from large companies but could be perfect for your start-up. The converse is true. A segment big enough to entice a large company, who have a large existing customer base and powerful unfair advantages, will be dangerous territory for a start-up.

On the other hand when a segment is 'too small' is easier to determine. If all the customers in the segment bought from you and you would still not be able to make a profit after expenses, it's too small! It's too small to generate enough profit to fuel growth. But, in your search for a repeatable and scalable business

you are likely to pivot several times on your way to 'success'. So if you can serve a customer and generate any revenue, it's better than none at all. Just make sure it's as a side project, not your full time job, and not costing you a lot of money.

Estimates are not a crystal ball. All back-of-the-envelope calculations are indicative not conclusive. Being in business is still the best way to be successful in business. To quote Walt Disney, "The best way to get started is to quit talking and begin doing." Pursue the opportunity but keep a flexible questioning attitude. If later you discover that the opportunity is too small, you can pivot taking the valuable experience gained with you to the next opportunity.

If you are serving an existing customer job and there are large incumbents, it may prove a challenge to conquer a large market share. All the more important to serve real customer jobs and delight customers! If, on the other hand, you are successful in an early market and find that established businesses with a lot more resources move in fast, pivoting is always an option. When incumbents consider an early market too small you will be safe from their swooping in. But it must be large enough to enable you to fuel your growth. If you find out that it is be too small even for you, pivot.

LEVEL UP TO
PRODUCT-
MARKET FIT

You've proven the existence of a problem and have designed a value proposition that addresses your customers' jobs, pains and gains. Your next stage of the start-up journey is at hand and it's time to give the big pivot or persevere question some thought.

If you feel this is a business you want to dedicate more time to persevere and start validating the business model and launch a minimal viable product.

If you feel this isn't the business for you then pivot, find the next thing you'll devote your energies too.

5

~ tools for working ~

Contents

6 value proposition pitches 188

Value proposition canvas 196

Experiment validation board 198

Test & learning cards 200

Business model canvas 202

6 VALUE PROPOSITION PITCHES
QUICK NAPKIN SKETCHES

If you can't easily explain why you exist, none of the subsequent steps matter. It's difficult to know where to start with writing a value proposition so we've collected a few templates to help exercise your value proposition crafting muscles. Your value proposition is like a gift to your customer. When you give a gift you think of what the receiver would enjoy. The same holds true for your value proposition. It is value from the perspective of the customer that counts.

ALEX OSTERWALDER'S ADLIBS

Example Our web platform helps educators in higher education who want to support students in reflective writing by reducing feedback time and increasing transparency unlike paper reflective practice journals.

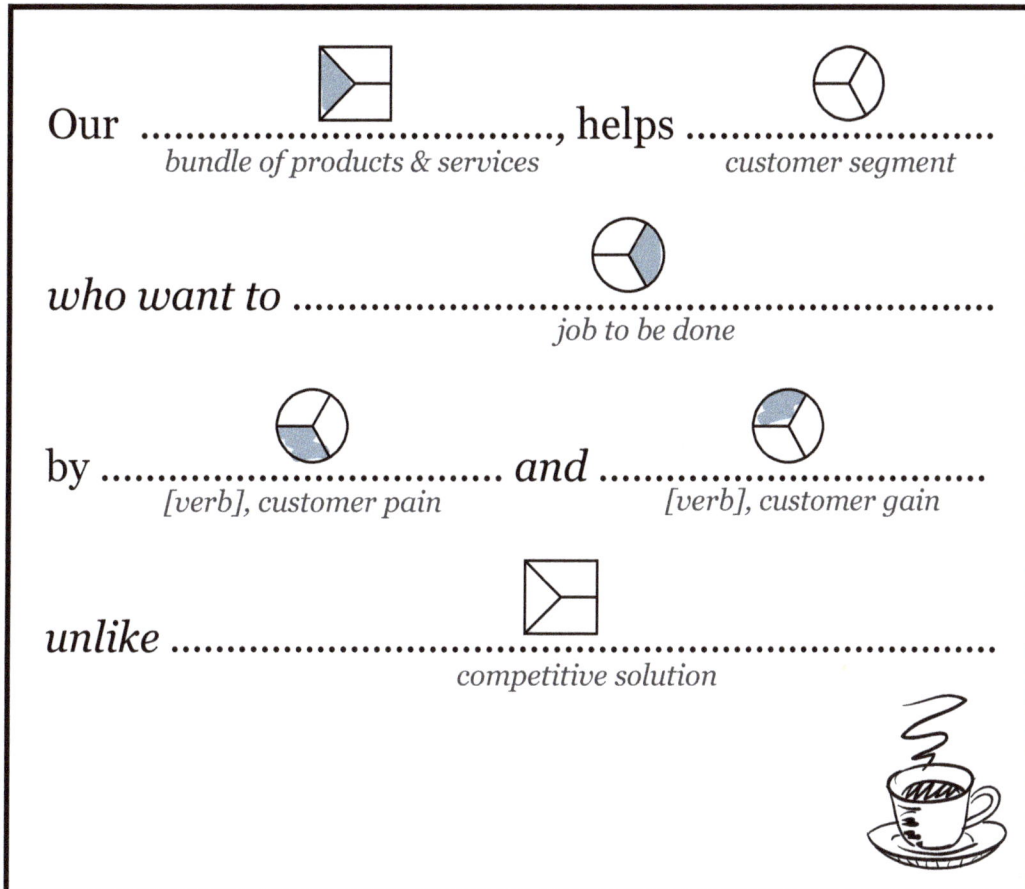

Our ...., helps ....
bundle of products & services   *customer segment*

who want to ....
job to be done

by .... and ....
[verb], customer pain   *[verb], customer gain*

unlike ....
competitive solution

Ad-libs force you to pinpoint how exactly you are going to create value.

DAVE MCCLURE'S ELEVATOR RIDE

Example Mint.com is the free, easy way to manage your money online.

· , ·
product name   *critical value created*

· ·
job to be done

GEOFF MOORE'S VALUE POSITIONING STATEMENT

Example For non-technical marketers who struggle to find return on investment in social media our web-based analytic software translates engagement metrics into actionable revenue metrics.

For .... who ....
     target customer   *need or opportunity*

our ....
                    product category

that ....
                    statement of benefit

STEVE BLANK'S XYZ

Example We help non-technical marketers improve and report return on investment in social media by turning engagement metrics into revenue metrics.

We help .... do ....
               target customer   *job to be done*

by doing ....
                      description of key benefit

THE FOUNDERS' INSTITUTE PITCH

Example We are developing a reflective practice web platform to help educators deepen student learning with our experience designing curricula in higher education.

We are developing ....,
defined offering

to help .... *solve* ..
target customer

.... with
problem

....
secret sauce (unfair advantage)

Avoid, 1) adjectives, particularly superlatives like "first," "only," "huge," or "best". These signal lack of awareness of the category. 2) generic segments like "women" or "small businesses". 3) buzzwords, acronyms or industry jargon. Keep it concise. It's easy to be wordy. In the words of Ernest Hemingway, "I don't have time to write you a short letter, so I'm writing you a long one." Take the time to hone your value statement.

CLAY CHRISTENSEN'S JOBS-TO-BE-DONE

Example

» Manage personal finances at home. (Mint.com)

» Preserving fun memories. (Kodak's Funsaver)

» Listen to music while jogging. (iPod)

...., ...
verb   *object*

....
context

VALUE PROPOSITION CANVAS
DEFINING VALUE

The **Value Proposition Canvas developed by Alexander Osterwalder and Yves Pigneur** zooms in, and describes in detail, the Customer Segment and the Value Proposition.

What is the *whole* MVP - the bundle of products & services your value proposition is built around? Products and services may be tangible (e.g. manufactured goods, face-to-face customer service), digital (e.g. downloads, online recommendations), intangible (e.g. copyrights), or financial (e.g. investment funds, financing services).

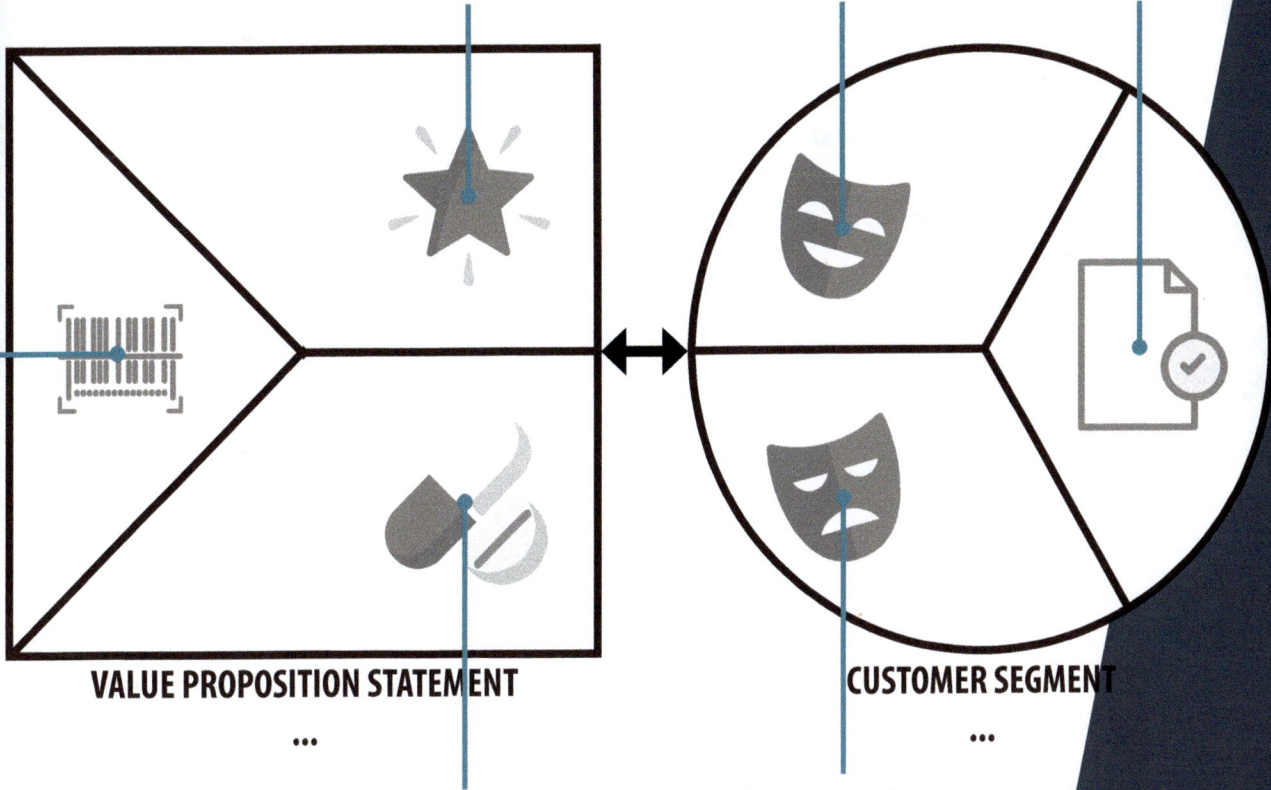

What features and characteristics of the MVP will create the expected and desired gains?

What benefits do customers minimally expect solutions to deliver? What benefits do customers desire - what would delight them?

What is the customers segments' most important functional job-to-get-done and are there concomitant emotional & social jobs?

VALUE PROPOSITION STATEMENT

•••

CUSTOMER SEGMENT

•••

What features and characteristics of the MVP will relieve the unwanted outcomes, obstacles to consumpotion and problems in use?

What unwanted outcomes and usage problems do customers experience when using current solutions? What impediments to consumption do they encounter?

EXPERIMENT VALIDATION BOARD
THE KEY TO DISCIPLINE

Writing test cards for all assumptions to be tested and placing them on a board for everyone in the team to see is a good way to make visible what is happening and the progress that you are making. The board has columns for, riskiest assumptions, experiment backlog, experiments under construction, running & learning.

» For each riskiest assumption you have identified, rewrite it as a hypothesis and capture it in this first column.

» Design a test card to (in)validate each of your hypotheses. Store them in the backlog column until you're ready to progress them.

» Depending on the test you've designed, the build stage could involve creating an interview, a landing page, a demo, or a functional prototype.

» Once your tests have been built enter the measuring phase where you capture data.

» When the experiment has run its course you can begin analysis. There are three possible outcomes from your analysis: uncertain = test more, validated = progress, or invalidated = pivot and review your hypotheses.

RISKIEST ASSUMPTIONS	BACKLOG	BUILD	MEASURE	LEARN

TEST & LEARNING CARDS
EXPERIMENT, EXPERIMENT

Define experiments to test your assumptions and capture insights gained in each test.

State the job-to-be-done, pain or gain assumption you are testing? If you are wrong, how critical a blow will this be to the business?

How will you test the assumption - interviews, smoke screens, or a working prototype? How reliable do you think this test will be?

What test metrics are you specifically measuring - emotional reaction, enthusiastic agreement, pre-sales inquiries, signups per 100?

Describe when you are satisfied the assumption is validated based on your metrics. For example, the number of interviewees that have a 7+ intensity on emotional response.

Note the date the card is created and the name of the person responsible.

TEST CARD

We believe that...

HYPOTHESIS   RISK HIGH MEDIUM LOW

To verify this we will...

TEST METHOD   RELIABILITY HIGH MEDIUM LOW

And measure...

METRICS

We are right when...

SUCCESS CRITERIA   HURDLE HIGH MEDIUM LOW

Date   **Who**

LEARNING CARD

We believed that...

HYPOTHESIS   RISK HIGH MEDIUM LOW

We observed...

OBSERVATION   RELIABILITY HIGH MEDIUM LOW

From that we learnt...

LEARNING & INSIGHT

Therefore, we will...

DECISION & ACTION   URGENCY HIGH MEDIUM LOW

Date   **Who**

What assumption were you testing?

Describe the results of the experiment and note how reliable you consider the result?

Describe what you have learnt from the the test. What conclusions can you make concerning the assumptions tested?

Will you persevere, pivot, or iterate based on the learnings? What is the business impact of the learnings and how urgently is action required?

Note the date of the learning the name of the person.

BUSINESS MODEL CANVAS
CREATE & DELIVER VALUE

The Business Model Canvas developed by Alexander Osterwalder and Yves Pigneur and originally published in *Business Model Generation* helps business strategists model a business using nine building blocks. Superficially, this is incredibly simply. It is to an extent, intuitive. Matters become complex when considering the interactions - from a helicopter view - between the building blocks. At the start, a business model is quite simple (especially when you don't know much yet), see the case study on *Reflectively*™. But as your knowledge about customers wants and needs grows so too will the detail and complexity in your business model grow. Do keep it a birds eye view and only get as complex as it needs to be. Keep in mind that less is often more. Making it complex, difficult to talk about and manage won't impress. Making it simple and intuitive itself might - but then again you don't need to impress anybody but you do need to keep a clear view on how you create, deliver and capture value for and from customers!

Who are you working closely with to create and deliver the value proposition?

Which activities must the business excel in to create and deliver value for each customer segment?

What is the bundle of products and services your value proposition is built around? What do customer value about it?

How will the business acquire customers? Why will they stay and why will they refer you to friends?

What is the initial customer segment? What is the critical functional job-to-be-done of your cookie monster?

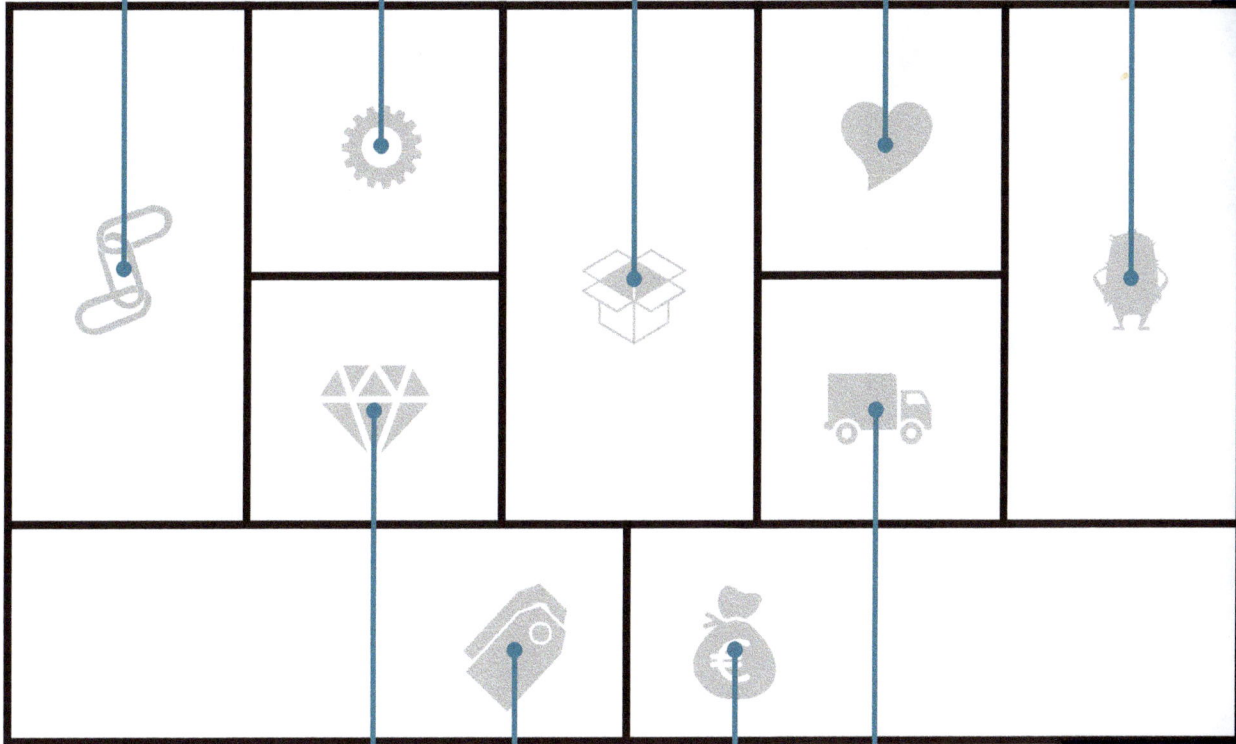

What intellectual, human, or physical resources do you have and need to create and deliver the proposition.

How will the business communicate with, sell, and deliver to customers?

What are the most important costs of the business model?

How does the business generate revenue (or value) off each segment?

6

~ end words ~

Contents

Terminology A - L   206

Terminology M - Z   207

Index   210

A - C

bootstrap

1. a loop of leather or cloth sewn at the top rear, or sometimes on each side, of a boot to facilitate pulling it on.

2. relying entirely on one's own efforts and resources to start a business.

3. to help (oneself) without the aid of others.

concierge

1. a hotel employee whose job is to assist guests by booking tours, making theatre and restaurant reservations, etc.

2. devoting your full attention to a single customer and tailoring the delivery of the value proposition by hand to meet their every need.

cookie monster

1. a character in the television show Sesame Street.

2. a customer with an acute job problem, who accepts rudimentary products and services and has budget.

business model

1. how a business creates, delivers and captures value.

customer job-to-be-done

1. the progress someone seeks to make in a specific context.

customer gains

1. the benefits and aspirations the customer seeks from the solution fre-

quently emotional and social

customer pains

1. the problems a customer experiences in relation to getting the job done.

2. the unwanted outcomes a customer experiences using current solutions.

3. the forces a customer experiences stopping them from from changing current behaviour or adopting a new solution.

customer problem

1. something that prevents a customer from making progress on the desired outcome.

earlyvangelist see *cookie monster*.

M - O

mechanical Turk also see *Wizard of Oz*

1. a chess playing automaton unveiled in 1770, operated by a hidden human player.

2. an MVP wherein the service is delivered to customers manually.

minimum viable product

1. a working product with the minimum of features that customers will pay for.

minimum marketable product see *minimal viable product.*

mosquito bite

    1.   a small customer problem.

offer

    1.   a value proposition, plus a demonstration, plus a price point.

pivot

    1.   a pin, point, or short shaft on the end of which something rests and turns, or upon and about which something rotates or oscillates.

    1.   a structured course correction designed to test a new fundamental hypothesis about the product, business model or engine of growth.

problem-solution fit

    1.   a validated customer problem and solution that solves the problem to the customers' satisfaction.

product-market fit

    1.   a validated business model with launching customers.

shark bite

    1.   a big customer problem.

solution

    1.   a value proposition, plus a minimal viable product, plus the customer experience.

traction

1. the grip of a tyre on a road or a wheel on a rail.

2. having proof of concept either through real sales or letters of intent from credible customers.

unicorn

1. a mythical animal typically represented as a horse with a single straight horn projecting from its forehead.

2. a startup valued at over one billion US dollars.

validate

1. to test an assumption for accuracy.

value proposition

1. a single arresting phrase that focuses on how your product or service solves customer problems and the tangible benefits customers can expect from using your products or services.

2. the bundle of products and services that constitute your solution and the characteristics (features) of the product that create gains and relieve customer pains.

wizard of Oz

1. the titular character in the book *The Wonderful Wizard of Oz.*

2. an MVP wherein the service is delivered to customers manually.

Index

A

additive manufacturing 45
Airbnb 32, 44
Amazon 36, 137
Apple 40
assumptions 65
  leap-of-faith 159
augmented intelligence 45
autonomous vehicles 45

B

big challenges 70
  organisational problems 70
  planetary challenges 39
  societal problems 70
blockchain 45
bootstrapping 37
brainstorming
  brainstorm solutions 136
  ideate applications 124
  painstorm problems 125
Brian Chesky 32
business model 137

C

company building 25
CRISPR 45
customer 68

buyer 69
cookie monster 82
  cookie monster profile 110, 122
decision maker 69
journey 176
user 69
watering holes 98
customer conversations
  advice interviews 107
  follow up questions 108
  problem validation 104
  three biggest problems 102
customer creation 25
customer development 25
customer discovery 25, 64
  problem-solution fit 83
customer gains 82, 121
customer jobs-to-be-done 71, 119
  clubeten, case study 154
  customer journey 176
  emotional jobs 72
  existing jobs 76
  functional jobs 72
  job context 72
  job statement 73
  job story 73
  new jobs 76
  social jobs 72
  underserved jobs 76, 78
customer pains 81, 120
customer problems
  mosquito bite 80

ranking bite size 118
shark bite 80
customer validation 25
product-market fit 184

D

Dan Norris 36
disruptive innovation 42
domain expertise 31

E

Elon Musk 39, 58
Evan Williams 34
experiments 86
experiment validation board 160
kill your darlings 160
learning card 160
methods, concierge 166
methods; demonstration 164
methods; mechanical Turk 166
methods, minimal viable product 167
methods; prototype 164
methods; smoke test 162
methods; wizard of Oz 166
planning experiments 160
test card 160

F

Facebook 32
founder drive cards
cause vision drive 52
customer pain drive 53
customer segment drive 57

problem drive 56
working moms, case study 100
product drive 50
technology drive 51
Google, case study 132
Frank Knight 28
freshwatching 142
calculatour, case study 144

G

general purpose technologies 44

H

hypotheses 65

I

innovation
disruptive innovation 42
revolutionary innovation 42

J

Jack Dorsey 34
Joe Gebbia 32
Joseph Schumpeter 24

L

learning velocity 65, 160

M

machine learning 45

market size
  serviceable available market 181
  serviceable obtainable market 181
  total available market 180
Mark Zuckerberg 32, 39
Matt Ruttledge 36
minimal viable product 167

N

Netflix 44, 74, 137
Noah Glass 34

P

PayPal 39
pivot 87
  Reflectively; case study 138
problem-solution fit 83
problem space 65
product-market fit 184
prototype 65, 164
  concierge 166
  mechanical Turk 166
  wizard of Oz 166

R

revenue model 44
robotics 45

S

safari
  customer problem 98

Salesforce 78, 137
segmentation
  customer segment 90
    zero in 116
  market segment 89
  minimum viable segment 179
Slack 32
small medium enterprise 24
solution 153
  desirable 42
  feasible 42
  viable 42
solution space 65
Space X 39, 58
Steve Jobs 40
Stewart Butterfield 32

T

Twitter 34

U

Uber 44

V

value proposition 143
  bundle of products & services 148
  club eten; case study 154
  design for delight 153
  gain creators 150
  pain relievers 149
  templates 188
  value map 148

W

Web Control Room 36
Woot.com 36
WP Curve 36

INFLUENCES AND INSPIRATION

BUSINESS MODEL GENERATION
Alexander Osterwalder and Yves Pigneur,
2008

BEYOND THE STARTUP MANIA
Jan-Willem van Beek and Rutger Huizinga,
2017

DESIGN A BETTER BUSINESS
Patrick van der Pijl, Justin Lokitz, and Lisa
Kay Soloman, 2016

DISCIPLINED ENTREPRENERUSHIP
Bill Aulet, 2013

SCALING LEAN
Ash Maurya, 2016

THE LEAN PRODUCT PLAYBOOK
Dan Olsen, 2010

REWORK
Jason Fried and David Heinemeier Hansson,
2010

THE LEADER'S GUIDE
Eric Ries, 2016

THE MOM TEST
Rob Fitzpatrick, 2013

VALUE PROPOSITION DESIGN
Alexander Osterwalder and Yves Pigneur,
2014

ACKNOWLEDGEMENTS

The path to this book was as twisty as the path of many a start-up. Over the years of production it's gone through several iterations. It started life as a reader created for a summer school program, then became a blog to be used in university programs, then a prototype book + workbook combination tested out with students over several seasons. The feedback received each iteration from students, educators and professionals were invaluable learning for the book you currently hold in your hands. I am deeply indebted to Barry Roberts, Carlos Nunez, Dick de Bruijn, Inge Boersma, Jolijn van Duijnhoven, Leewee Chew, Marcellien Breedveld, Maurice Brown, Norbert Vincent, Roland Wijnen, Shaikh Khalid Raihan, Tijs Markusse, and Yoram Spreij for reviewing concepts, spreads, sections, chapters, for their support, and for conversations that encouraged and inspired me to persevere.

ABOUT

Robert de Bruijn is a lecturer and education designer at HU University of Applied Sciences, Utrecht. He develops and runs experiential learning programs on entrepreneurship, strategic marketing and innovation. After a career spanning more than a decade in digital product management and marketing he launched a first venture in 2005 as a side project, but shelved the project after two years of operation due to scalability issues. A second venture, launched in 2008, taught more valuable lessons in a month about entrepreneurship and vigorously validating assumptions than the first venture did in two years. His current projects include a digital education platform fit for 21st century learning and development. He is passionate about education and is convinced of each persons ability to unlock their creativity. Connect with Robert on Twitter @robertdebruijn or LinkedIn rkddebruijn.

www.ingramcontent.com/pod-product-compliance
Lightning Source LLC
Chambersburg PA
CBHW050344230326
41458CB00102B/6351